WRIT OF HABEAS CORPUS MANUAL

28 U.S.C. § 2254 Habeas Corpus Practice Manual, Case Law & Forms

The Essential Guide for:

- Learning the Roadmap to Take Your Case to Federal Court
- Understanding Habeas Corpus Law and How it Applies to You
- Drafting Comprehensive Legal Arguments
- A Plethora of Relevant Case Law to Use in Your Petition
- Writing a Compelling Petition for a Writ of Habeas Corpus
- Properly Presenting Your Claims to the Federal District Court
- Raising Your Claims to the U.S. Circuit Court of Appeals

Tear & Share To Order Manual	Tear & Share To Order Manual	Tear & Share To Order Manual
SCAN ME	SCAN ME	SCAN ME

CEDRIC MARTIN HOPKINS, ESQ.

P.O. Box 213
Woodland, CA 95776
objectionyourhonor@hotmail.com

A NOTE ABOUT COPYRIGHT LAW AND THIS MANUAL

The copyright to this Manual is protected vigorously and all infringements will be pursued to the fullest extent of the law.

The Manual should have been purchased by you or for you, directly. Any copying of any of the pages, or parts thereof, in this Manual (other than those the author has given permission to copy) is strictly prohibited. This Manual, or any parts thereof, may not be reproduced in any form without permission in writing from the author.

For information, contact: objectionyourhonor@hotmail.com.

TOP COPYRIGHT MYTHS:

- **Everything on the Internet is 'public domain' and free to use.**

  FALSE: Works on the Internet are publicly accessible but are not in the 'public domain' as it pertains to copyright laws. A work is only considered in the 'public domain' (and thereby free to use without any infringement) when the copyright expires.

- **Any work without a copyright notice is not protected.**

  FALSE: Prior to January 1, 1978, this was true. Since that date, copyright protection attaches as soon as the author's idea is put into tangible form.

- **If I change someone else's work I can claim it as my own.**

  FALSE: Simply changing someone else's work is a prohibited act. Any adaptation will be legally regarded as a 'derived work' and will still be considered the original author's work.

- **It's okay to use another person's work if I don't make money from it.**

  FALSE: Unless you have permission to do so, you cannot use another's work regardless if you make money or not from the use of the work. And with respect to this specific Manual, you need written permission from the author to use any portion of the work.

- **I can copy 10% of a work without it constituting infringement.**

  FALSE: Any unauthorized copying, publication or use of a copyrighted work is strictly prohibited and is infringement.

HOW TO USE THIS MANUAL

If you're reading this then more than likely you are (1) sitting in a prison you don't want to be in, (2) serving time you don't want to be serving and (3) needing to write a petition for writ of habeas corpus that you may not know how to write. This Manual was written to assist you with number 3, which will hopefully help you out with 1 and 2.

Several forms have been provided with this Manual. The provided forms are essential in properly preparing a pro per petition for writ of habeas corpus. The forms will help you organize your petition and offer you a more professional look and feel to the pleadings that you will need to file with the court during the federal writ process.

It is often said that a petition for writ of habeas corpus carries more weight if an attorney files it. That may be somewhat true. Another truth, however, is that a well-written petition (from an attorney or inmate) is highly valued by judges.

In my time clerking for a judge, I reviewed a number of petitions, motions or other pleadings, some from attorneys, others from inmates. There was a consensus among all of the law clerks I worked with: we didn't care who wrote the petition, as long as it was well organized and to the point.

Some attorneys know how to organize their pleadings and write in a clear, concise manner while still making a strong, persuasive point. Others don't. The issue for inmates is that their pleadings are far too often unorganized and mix points of law with each other, which often waters down the power of their pleadings. This Manual provides guidance to writing a powerful petition—one that will not only be read and understood by the judge, but will be effective and persuasive, as well.

Some of the forms provided may be copied and used multiple times. Some of the forms have lines for your writing and others do not. Some forms (like the pro per petition for writ of habeas corpus) don't have lines for your writing because there would be too many lines on the pages, which would be a distraction for the reader.

HINT: For the forms that do not have lines you should use a piece of paper as a straight edge and lightly pencil in lines, write your petition in ink (black, NOT blue) using those light pencil lines and then go back and erase the pencil lines. This will make your petition (and other pleadings you file) have a more finished look to them.

ATTORNEY-CLIENT RELATIONSHIP

No attorney-client relationship exists by the purchase of this Manual. This Manual is provided as an explanation of petitions for writ of habeas corpus and a roadmap to help you navigate through the writ process. This Manual does not, in any way, create an attorney-client relationship with anyone who purchases it or receives it.

The information and tips in this Manual are suggestions only and do not have to be followed blindly. You are free to use your own techniques and pull from this Manual what you feel is beneficial to preparing a successful petition for writ of habeas corpus. You are in no way bound, compelled or forced to use the suggestions made in this Manual.

In order for you to form an attorney-client relationship with the author of this Manual, a written and signed retainer agreement needs to be in place.

TABLE OF CONTENTS

1. WHAT IS A WRIT OF HABEAS CORPUS?

Habeas corpus literally means, "you shall have the body," or person, in court. A writ is a formal order under seal issued by a court. So a writ of habeas corpus is a court order that requires a person who has been detained to appear in court to decide whether their incarceration is legal or not.

You are filing a petition for a writ of habeas corpus. So what you are doing is petitioning the federal district court for an order (writ) to bring you back into court (habeas corpus) to determine if your conviction and/or sentence are valid. That's why it's called a petition for writ of habeas corpus. You may hear it called, "Petition for Writ," or "Writ," or "The Great Writ," or "Habeas Corpus," or simply, "Habeas." It's all the same thing.

For the historians reading this, the writ of habeas corpus has its origins in English common law from the Middle Ages. It's impossible to pinpoint when it was initially written down, but it was most famously enshrined in the 1215 Magna Carta, which guaranteed all free men protection against arbitrary incarceration. This English legislation was brought to the British colonies in North America. In turn, the Magna Carta impacted the US Constitution.

Article I, Section 9 of the United States Constitution states, "The privilege of the Writ of Habeas Corpus shall not be suspended, unless when in Cases of Rebellion or Invasion the public Safety may require it."

Alexander Hamilton wrote in his Federalist Paper No. 84, "The establishment of the writ of habeas corpus, the prohibition of ex post facto laws...are perhaps greater securities to liberty and republicanism than any [the Constitution] contains."

And Thomas Jefferson called the protections provided by habeas corpus one of the "essential principles of our Government."

A. 2241 vs. 2255 vs. 2254

Depending on the procedural posture of your case, a certain U.S. Code section will control your habeas corpus process. While this Manual is focused on Section 2254 (state convictions being challenged in federal court), you may hear other sections of the U.S. Code mentioned. Here's a brief overview of what those other U.S. Code sections are for your information:

28 U.S.C. Sec. 2241

A motion under 28 U.S.C. Sec. 2241 is a legal procedure that allows someone to petition about being wrongfully held in prison for specific legal reasons. Some of those reasons are as follows:

- You are a federal prisoner and you wish to challenge the way your sentence is being carried out (for example, you claim that the Bureau of Prisons miscalculated your sentence or failed to properly award good time credits);
- You are in federal or state custody because of something other than a judgment of conviction (for example, you are in pretrial detention or are awaiting extradition); or
- You are alleging that you are illegally detained in immigration custody; or
- There is an issue at the prison that has been unsuccessfully resolved by the Bureau of Prisons' Administrative Remedies Program after all other options have been exhausted (meaning after the BP-9, BP-10, and BP-11 forms have been filed and denied).

28 U.S.C. Sec. 2255

Section 2255 applies to inmates **who were convicted in federal court** and are serving their prison sentence in federal prison. This is different than inmates who were convicted in state court and serving their prison sentence in state court. For inmates who were convicted in federal court, they must use the procedures under 28 U.S.C. Sec. 2255 to collaterally attack their conviction. This collateral attack is usually done after the direct appeal in federal court is completed.

The long form of the title of the 2255 motion is, "Motion Under 28 U.S.C. § 2255 to Vacate, Set Aside, or Correct Sentence by a Person in Federal Custody." It is commonly referred to as a "collateral attack on the judgment," as opposed to a direct appeal, which is a "direct attack on the judgment." It is a type of post-conviction motion. The various States also have laws governing state post-conviction relief petitions, which differ from the post-conviction relief federal motion in Section 2255.

Motions filed pursuant to 28 U.S.C. Sec. 2255 typically address the following issues for those inmates convicted in federal court:

(1) Ineffective assistance of counsel at the plea, trial, sentencing, and/or appeal levels. If an attorney representing the defendant was "ineffective" within the legal meaning of that word, then it must be complained of in a 2255 motion.

(2) Prosecutorial misconduct. If the U.S. Attorney's office or an agent of the Government committed "misconduct" within the legal meaning of that word, and that affected the defendant's substantial rights and, except for that conduct, there would have been a different result in the case, then it must be raised in a 2255 motion.

(3) Newly discovered evidence. If, after sentencing, there is new evidence discovered that could not have been discovered before the sentencing, you may raise that in a 2255 motion.

This issue cannot be raised in a direct appeal because the review on appeal is limited to the record that existed at the time the sentence was imposed. (Ineffective assistance of counsel and prosecutorial misconduct cannot be raised in a direct appeal either.)

(4) A substantive change to the law that has been explicitly made retroactive by the U.S. Supreme Court.

28 U.S.C. Sec. 2254

This is the U.S. Code section that this Manual is specifically designed to help guide you through. Although, even if you are filing a motion under 2255, this Manual could also help you write compelling and persuasive arguments when preparing that motion, as well.

Section 2254 applies to inmates who were convicted in state court. Section 2254 allows those inmates to have their state conviction and sentence reviewed for error by the federal courts. When you file a petition for a writ of habeas corpus under 28 U.S.C. Sec. 2254 as a state convicted inmate, you are challenging the validity of a state judgment of conviction and sentence. This means that your criminal case did not originate in federal court; your case started in state court.

As explained in detail below, by filing a petition for a writ of habeas corpus under Section 2254, an inmate can challenge the way the state courts decided federal issues that were exhausted in the state court appellate system. Drafting Section 2254 petitions is complex due to the legal requirements that need to be met with several legal concepts. This Manual was written to strip away that complexity and provide the pro per litigant with straightforward guidelines and insightful tips that will produce a petition that will be read, effective and persuasive.

B. STATE COURT VS. FEDERAL COURT

It's important to understand the differences between state court and federal court. This Manual was intended to assist inmates who were convicted in state court and now want to take their case to federal court.

The table below compares the two court systems (state vs. federal):

State Court System	Federal Court System
The Constitution and laws of each state establish the state courts. A court of last resort, often known as a Supreme Court, is usually the highest court in the state. Some states also have an intermediate Court of Appeals. Below these appeals courts, are the state trial	Article III of the Constitution invests the judicial power of the United States in the federal court system. Article III, Section 1 specifically creates the U.S. Supreme Court and gives Congress the authority to create the lower federal

courts. Some are referred to as Superior Courts, Circuit Courts or District Courts.	courts.
States also usually have courts (or sometimes called "benches") that handle specific legal matters, e.g., criminal court, probate court (wills and estates); juvenile court; family court; etc. Judges often rotate through these different courts or benches.	Congress has used this power to establish the 13 U.S. Courts of Appeals, the 94 U.S. District Courts, the U.S. Court of Claims, and the U.S. Court of International Trade. U.S. Bankruptcy Courts handle bankruptcy cases. Magistrate Judges handle some District Court matters, including habeas corpus petitions.
Parties dissatisfied with the decision of the trial court may take their case to the intermediate State Court of Appeals.	Parties dissatisfied with a decision of a U.S. District Court, the U.S. Court of Claims, and/or the U.S. Court of International Trade may appeal to a U.S. Court of Appeals of one of the 13 Circuits.
Parties have the option to ask the highest state court to hear the case.	A party may ask the U.S. Supreme Court to review a decision of the U.S. Court of Appeals, but the Supreme Court usually is under no obligation to do so. The U.S. Supreme Court is the final arbiter of federal constitutional questions.
Only certain cases are eligible for review by the U.S. Supreme Court.	

As you will learn through this Manual, you cannot go to federal court until you meet a few conditions. Once those conditions are met, then you can move your case from the state court system to the federal court system.

I have felt that appellants such as you get a more objective look at the issues they are presenting in federal court rather than in state court. The federal court system is deciding the federal issues in your case and making sure the state court decided those issues correctly. Therefore, the federal court wants to ensure that their body of law is accurately resolved.

2. PRELIMINARY MATTERS TO ADDRESS BEFORE PREPARING YOUR PETITION

Typically with appellate proceedings there is a notice that you are required to file with the court before you proceed with your appeal or post-conviction matter. For direct appeals following a trial you file a notice of appeal before a certain deadline. For post-conviction relief proceedings you file a notice of post-conviction relief with the court in order to begin your post-conviction relief proceedings.

With federal habeas proceedings, you do not need to file such a notice. There is no notice to file with the federal or state court before you file the petition. Your federal habeas proceedings don't start until you file a petition for a writ of habeas corpus.

There are a few preliminary matters that need to be addressed, however, before you start to prepare the petition. The next few sections will explain, in detail, what those preliminary matters are and help you understand how they fit into your particular situation.

A. GETTING YOUR CASE STARTED

Before you can bring your case from state court to federal district court, your case must meet a couple of critical conditions. If you cannot meet these conditions, then the federal district court is likely to reject your petition for a writ of habeas corpus. In order to start your federal case in federal district court, you must be within one year of your state proceedings ending and you must have exhausted your claims in state court.

CRITICAL TIP: These two concepts – statute of limitations and exhaustion – are critical concepts that you should focus on prior to drafting your petition (while your state proceedings are ongoing) and while drafting your petition for a writ of habeas corpus. These will be the first couple of sections that the prosecutor's office and district court judge focus on because they are the easy way to dismiss your petition.

B. TIMELINE TO FILE YOUR PETITION FOR WRIT OF HABEAS CORPUS

1. STATUTE OF LIMITATIONS

Generally speaking, you get one year to file the petition for a writ of habeas corpus. Through the code sections explained below, however, that one-year time period doesn't typically start until you have finished challenging your state conviction and sentence.

28 U.S.C. Sec. 2244

28 U.S.C. Sec. 2244 controls the timeline (deadline) for you to file the petition for writ of habeas corpus. Here is the actual statute that controls the timeline:

28 U.S.C. Sec. 2244(d)(1) A 1-year period of limitation shall apply to an application for a writ of habeas corpus by a person in custody pursuant to the judgment of a State court. The limitation period shall run from the latest of—

(A) The date on which the judgment became final by the conclusion of direct review or the expiration of the time for seeking such review;

(B) The date on which the impediment to filing an application created by State action in violation of the Constitution or laws of the United States is removed, if the applicant was prevented from filing by such State action;

(C) The date on which the constitutional right asserted was initially recognized by the Supreme Court, if the right has been newly recognized by the Supreme Court and made retroactively applicable to cases on collateral review; or

(D) The date on which the factual predicate of the claim or claims presented could have been discovered through the exercise of due diligence.

So, 28 U.S.C. Sec. 2244(d)(1) tells you when to start the clock for the statute of limitations (deadline to file the petition). You may see this section of the Code and feel that your time has already passed. It is likely, however, that you have more time to file your habeas petition than you realize.

a. Tolling

Tolling means that a statute of limitation stops running for a certain period of time.

"Statutory" tolling means that the tolling is governed by statute, as opposed to "equitable" tolling, discussed below, which is governed by case law only. The habeas corpus statute provides tolling for a state prisoner while he or she completes state court proceedings on a "properly filed application for State post-conviction or other collateral review with respect to the pertinent judgment or claim." 28 U.S.C. 2244(d)(2).

Unlike many other statutes of limitation, the one-year federal habeas corpus statute of limitations can start and stop several times, depending on whether state court collateral filings are pending or concluded. However, when it starts again, it does not start over with a full year remaining. It is important to note that the days that go by (1) between the final judgment and a collateral filing, and (2)between final disposition of a collateral filing and the federal habeas corpus filing, count against the year. *Nino v. Galaza*, 183 F.3d 1003, 1006-07 (9th Cir. 1999).

For example, if John Doe's direct appeal becomes final by an opinion or remittitur from the state court, and John Doe waits 355 days after the date of finality to file a state collateral review proceeding, such as a post-conviction notice, then he has used up 355 days of his federal habeas corpus statute of limitations under 28 U.S.C. § 2244(d)(1). The filing of the state collateral review application will statutorily toll or stop John Doe's federal habeas corpus statute of limitations while the state collateral review proceeding is pending, through appeal of that action to the state appellate system.

When that action is final, John Doe's one-year federal habeas corpus statute of limitations will start running again, but the "clock" is not reset at one year, it starts at the number of days left. In this example, John Doe would have only 10 days in which to file his federal habeas corpus petition because he used 355 days between the direct appeal and the first state collateral challenge.

It is important to know that only "properly-filed" state court post-conviction or other collateral review applications will toll the federal habeas corpus statute of limitations. In *Artuz v. Bennett*, 531 U.S. 4 (2000), the United States Supreme Court determined that a properly filed application that tolls the statute of limitation is defined as follows:

An application is "filed," as that term is commonly understood, when it is delivered to, and accepted by, the appropriate court officer for placement into the official record .... And an application is "properly filed" when its delivery and acceptance are in compliance with the applicable laws and rules governing filings. These usually prescribe, for example, the form of the document, the time limits upon its delivery, the court and office in which it must be lodged, and the requisite filing fee.

A post-conviction petition that has been dismissed by the state court as untimely under state law is not a properly-filed one for purposes of § 2244(d)(2). *Pace v. Diguglielmo*, 544 U.S. 408, 417 (2005).

If the federal court finds that a prior state court action was improperly filed, that state court action will not be deemed to have tolled or stopped the statute of limitations, and the federal court may deem the federal petition untimely, as a result. Moreover, prior federal habeas corpus petitions dismissed without prejudice do not toll or stop the statute of limitation for a later petition. *Duncan v. Walker*, 533 U.S. 167, 182 (2001).

28 U.S.C. Sec. 2244(d)(2)

Section 2244(d)(2) is the subsection of the Federal Code that allows you to toll (temporarily stop) the statute of limitations period. Here is the actual subsection of the Code that controls tolling of deadline to file the habeas petition:

Section 2244(d)(2) "The time during which a properly filed application for State post-conviction or other collateral review with respect to the pertinent judgment or claim is pending shall not be counted toward any period of limitation under this subsection."

What Section 2244(d)(2) is allowing you to do is pause the statute of limitations clock while you are fighting your conviction and sentence in state court appellate proceedings.

State Court Proceedings

Your case started in state court. You were arrested for a crime, went to jail, proceeded through your case and ended up accepting a plea agreement or were found guilty at trial. This was all done in a court called "superior court" or "state circuit court" or "state district court." The time to file your federal habeas corpus petition did not start during those proceedings.

REMEMBER: The word "district" is also used in the federal system, but those courts are called "Federal District Court," and will be associated with the area in which they are located. For example, one of the federal district courts in California is the United States District Court for the Eastern District of California. These federal district courts are where federal defendants handle their cases. Your case was in a state court, not one of these federal courts.

The process is somewhat different for those defendants who plead guilty versus those who went to trial to challenge their state court cases. Without knowing your specific state's laws, the idea is generally the same from state to state with respect to challenging convictions, as explained below.

b. Pleading Defendants

If you chose to accept a plea agreement and waived your right to a trial, then you likely waived your right to file a direct appeal to the state court of appeals. The manner in which defendants who have accepted a plea agreement can challenge their conviction and sentence is through state post-conviction relief proceedings.

For example, in Arizona, those proceedings are governed by post-conviction of the Arizona Rules of Procedure and allow a defendant to argue ineffective assistance of counsel claims, among many other claims, to challenge the plea agreement, conviction, prison sentence, or a number of other issues that may have come up during their case. These challenges are typically called "collateral attacks" on the conviction.

These post-conviction relief proceedings typically are first heard in the court of origin (in the court you were convicted in and by the judge who sentenced you).

If you are not successful in challenging your conviction before the court of origin, then you typically are able to seek review of that decision in the state court of appeals. You seek review by filing what is usually called a "petition for review" with the state court of appeals. This is similar to an appeal after being found guilty following a trial, but this petition for review only can raise issues that are associated with the collateral attack you presented as part of your post-conviction relief case.

If you are not successful in the state court of appeals with a petition for review, then you can seek review of the court of appeals' decision by filing a petition for further review with the state supreme court.

So long as you are timely seeking review of the decisions made by the superior court and the court of appeals, then the time to file your federal petition for writ of habeas corpus has not started yet.

Once you have received the final order in your state court appellate proceedings affirming your conviction and sentence, then the clock starts for you to file the federal petition for writ of habeas corpus.

c. Non-Pleading Defendants

If you did not accept a plea agreement and chose to exercise your right to a jury trial or bench trial (trial before the judge, not the jury), then you likely retained your right to seek direct review of your conviction and sentence with the state court of appeals. For non-pleading defendants, you will have the opportunity to have the state court of appeals review nearly all aspects of your case, from beginning to end.

Typically, you file a notice of appeal following your conviction and sentence. The notice of appeal indicates that you are seeking review of your case in the state court of appeals. If you are not successful in the state court of appeals, then you likely can file in the state supreme court for review of the state court of appeals' decision.

Once you have sought direct review of your case in the highest state court, non-pleading defendants in most states can then seek to collaterally attack their conviction and sentence in the superior court. As explained above in the "Pleading Defendants" section, the collateral attack is typically called state post-conviction relief proceedings.

Once the collateral attacks on the conviction and sentence is completed (as explained above in the "Pleading Defendants" section), then the clock starts running for the deadline to file the federal petition for writ of habeas corpus.

d. 90-Day Rule

If a direct appeal was filed and pursued through the state court system, the one-year statute of limitation does not start until expiration of the additional 90-day period "within which [a petitioner] could have filed a petition for a writ of certiorari from the United States Supreme Court" following direct appeal, whether or not one was filed. *Bowen v. Roe*, 188 F.3d 1157, 1159 (9th Cir.1999).

If you seek review in the U.S. Supreme Court by filing a petition for writ of certiorari, then your conviction becomes final when the U.S. Supreme Court decides your petition.

If you do not seek review in the U.S. Supreme Court, then your conviction becomes final 90 days after the highest state court decides your case. The 90-day rule means that your time to file your federal petition for writ of habeas corpus is tolled during the time you have to seek review in the U.S. Supreme Court (90 days).

CRITICAL TIP: Please note that the additional 90-day certiorari period, however, does not apply to post-conviction relief actions, and so do not count that time period into your federal statute of limitations calculation. The 90-day rule applies to direct appeals only.

Remember: You have one year to file your federal petition for writ of habeas corpus under 28 U.S.C. Sec. 2254 in federal district court once your state-court conviction and sentence becomes final. Make sure to seek timely review of your state-court conviction and sentence in state court so that the time to file your federal petition for writ of habeas corpus is tolled. If there is any question if you are going to be late filing the habeas petition, file it immediately. You can amend the petition at a later date.

e. Equitable Tolling

If you think you missed your statute of limitations deadline, you may ask the Court to toll the limitations period for fairness reasons, a concept known as "equitable tolling." However,"the threshold necessary to trigger equitable tolling [under AEDPA] is very high, lest the exceptions swallow the rule." *Miranda v. Castro*, 292 F.3d 1063, 1066 (9th Cir. 2002).

To qualify for equitable tolling, the petitioner bears the burden of proving two elements: (1) that he was pursuing his rights diligently during the entire time that he seeks to have tolled, and (2) that some extraordinary circumstance stood in his or her way, preventing him from filing a habeas petition in a timely manner. *Holland v. Florida*, 130 S. Ct. 2549, 2562 (2010).

If you wish to make an argument for equitable tolling, you should provide all of the facts necessary for the Court to make this determination, including affidavits and any written documentation you have that supports your argument that you were diligently pursuing your rights during the statute of limitations period, but that an extraordinary circumstance actually prevented you from filing your habeas petition on time.

2. EXHAUSTION RULE AND PROCEDURAL DEFAULTS

The exhaustion rule and procedural default sections are being discussed together because they are related in form, as shown below. The U.S. Supreme Court and circuit courts of appeal have repeatedly explained and decided the exhaustion rule and procedural defaults.

The exhaustion rule means that you have to pursue all remedies that would be available to you in state court before bringing your case to federal court. If you fail to exhaust all possible remedies in state court, then you are procedurally defaulted from raising those claims in federal court. "Procedurally defaulted" simply means that there is no avenue for you to get into federal court.

The U.S. Supreme Court stated it as follows:

"The habeas statute generally requires a state prisoner to exhaust state remedies before filing a habeas petition in federal court. See 28 U.S.C. §§ 2254(b)(1), (c). "This rule of comity reduces friction between the state and federal court systems by avoiding the 'unseem[liness]' of a federal district court's overturning a state-court conviction without the state courts having had an opportunity to correct the constitutional violation in the first instance." *O'Sullivan v. Boerckel*, 526 U.S. 838, 845, 119 S. Ct. 1728, 144 L. Ed. 2d 1 (1999) (alteration in original). A state prisoner is generally barred from obtaining federal habeas relief unless the prisoner has properly presented his or her claims through one "complete round of the State's established appellate review process." Ibid. In practical terms, the law of habeas, like administrative law, requires proper exhaustion, and we have described this feature of habeas law as follows: "To . . . 'protect the integrity' of the federal exhaustion rule, we ask not only whether a prisoner has exhausted his state remedies, but also whether he has properly exhausted those remedies . . . ." Id., at 848, 119 S. Ct. 1728, 144 L. Ed. 2d 1." *Woodford v. Ngo*, 548 U.S. 81, 92-93 (2006).

"The law of habeas, however, uses terminology that differs from that of administrative law. In habeas, the sanction for failing to exhaust properly (preclusion of review in federal court) is given the separate name of procedural default, although the habeas doctrines of exhaustion and procedural default ' are similar in purpose and design and implicate similar concerns," *Keeney v. Tamayo-Reyes*, 504 U.S. 1, 7, 112 S. Ct. 1715, 118 L. Ed. 2d 318 (1992).

“In habeas, state-court remedies are described as having been "exhausted" when they are no longer available, regardless of the reason for their unavailability. *See Gray v. Netherland*, 518 U.S. 152, 161, 116 S. Ct. 2074, 135 L. Ed. 2d 457 (1996). Thus, if state-court remedies are no longer available because the prisoner failed to comply with the deadline for seeking state-court review or for taking an appeal, those remedies are technically exhausted, ibid., but exhaustion in this sense does not automatically entitle the habeas petitioner to litigate his or her claims in federal court. Instead, if the petitioner procedurally defaulted those claims, the prisoner generally is barred from asserting those claims in a federal habeas proceeding.” Id., at 162, 116 S. Ct. 2074, 135 L. Ed. 2d 457; *See Coleman v. Thompson*, 501 U.S. 722, 744-751, 111 S. Ct. 2546, 115 L. Ed. 2d 640 (1991).

In other words, what the U.S. Supreme Court is telling you is that you must present all of your claims in state court and pursue your remedies there before bringing your claims to federal court. If you fail to do so, then your claims will be subject to procedural default.

Your claims may be precluded if you failed to properly present the claims in State court and returning your case to State court to do so would be “futile” because of the State court’s procedural rules—such as waiver or preclusion in filing a successive post-conviction petition—would bar the State court from considering the previously unraised claims. *Teague v. Lane*, 489 U.S. 288, 297-299 (1989).

Your federal claim may also be procedurally barred if, despite properly raising the federal claim in State court, the State court found the claim barred on State procedural grounds. *Beard v. Kindler*, 558 U.S. 53 (2009). So your federal claims will be barred if the State court relied “on a state-law ground that is both ‘independent’ of the merits of the federal claim and an ‘adequate’ basis for the court’s decision.” *Harris v. Reed*, 489 U.S. 255, 260 (1989).

A state procedural ruling is “independent” if the application of the bar does not depend on an antecedent ruling on the merits of the federal claim. And it is “adequate” if it is “strictly or regularly followed.” *Wells v. Maass*, 28 F.3d 1005, 1010 (9th Cir. 1994).

Despite all of these procedural default rules, which are designed to bar your federal claims, federal courts retain the power to consider the merits of procedurally defaulted claims. *Reed v. Ross*, 468 U.S. 1, 9 (1984). Typically, a federal court will not review the merits of a procedurally defaulted claim unless you demonstrate “cause” for the failure to properly exhaust the claim in State court and “prejudice” from the alleged constitutional violation, or you show that a “fundamental miscarriage of justice” would result if the claim were not heard on the merits. *Coleman v. Thompson*, 501 U.S. 722, 750 (1991). But be careful, because the federal court also holds the power to dismiss plainly meritless claims regardless of whether the claim was properly exhausted in State court. *Rhines v. Weber*, 544 U.S. 269, 277 (2005).

But what happens if you failed to exhaust your remedies in state court? The Ninth Circuit Court of Appeals has answered that question this way:

"The Supreme Court has noted that a habeas petitioner who has defaulted his federal claims in state court meets the technical requirements for exhaustion; there are no state remedies any longer available to him. In cases such as this, where a petitioner did not properly exhaust state remedies and the court to which the petitioner would be required to present his claims in order to meet the exhaustion requirement would now find the claims procedurally barred, the petitioner's claim is procedurally defaulted. In light of the procedural bar to Smith returning to state court to exhaust his state remedies properly, the relevant question becomes whether Smith's procedural default can be excused, not whether Smith's failure to exhaust can be excused. Therefore, the exceptions to the exhaustion requirement set forth in § 2254(b) are irrelevant to Smith's petition. Rather, we must determine whether we can excuse Smith's procedural default under the applicable exception to that rule." *Smith v. Baldwin*, 510 F.3d 1127, 1139 (9th Cir. 2007); *see also Cooper v. Neven*, 641 F.3d 322, 327 (9th Cir. 2011).

So if your claims are considered procedurally defaulted, then you will need to convince the federal district court to consider your claims anyway. The U.S. Supreme Court explained how to meet that burden: "...federal review of the claims is barred unless the prisoner can demonstrate cause for the default and actual prejudice as a result of the alleged violation of federal law, or demonstrate that failure to consider the claims will result in a fundamental miscarriage of justice." *Coleman*, 501 U.S. at 750.

So as the *Coleman* decision shows, you have to address two issues to get around the procedural default: 1) cause for the default, and 2) actual prejudice as a result of the alleged violation of federal law.

If you are not able to properly address those two issues, then you can use the "fundamental miscarriage of justice" option and argue that the federal district court should hear your case because if it fails to do so, then there will be a fundamental miscarriage of justice.

C. Claims That Are Proper For A Petition for a Writ of Habeas Corpus

The general rule is that only issues related to federal constitutional violations may be raised in a 2254 petition for a writ of habeas corpus. The federal district court will not consider issues that are based solely on your state's laws. The federal courts are only concerned with making sure the state courts decide their federal issues correctly.

Also, the federal court cannot consider any claims that were not first presented to the highest state court in your state. That means you must first exhaust all of your claims by presenting them, with citations to governing federal authority, to both the intermediate appellate court in your state, along with the supreme court in your state, before bringing your claims to federal court through a 2254 petition for a writ of habeas corpus. As explained in the previous section (Section (2)(B)(2)), you must first exhaust all of your potential claims in state court before proceeding to federal court.

1. **Federal Issues in State Cases**

When you were charged with crimes, the crimes were based on your state's laws. Those state laws were litigated in court and you either accepted a plea agreement or exercised your right to a trial. Either way, you were operating under the laws of your state.

At the same time, however, the United States Constitution and some federal statutes were also controlling your case. You may not have heard those federal issues raised in court, but they were protecting you nonetheless.

For example, the Sixth Amendment to the United States Constitution requires that your defense attorney provide you with effective assistance of counsel. If your defense attorney provided you with ineffective assistance of counsel, then you may have a claim to raise in federal court with a petition for a writ of habeas corpus. But if you want to raise a claim to the specific state law your were convicted of while having that ineffective lawyer, that issue would not be properly brought in a habeas corpus petition. So, in other words, the legal claims in the habeas corpus petition have to be grounded in your rights ensured by the United States Constitution or federal statutes.

The benefit of proceeding to federal court if you don't get relief in state court is that the federal court is not concerned with state law or how the state courts decided cases or issues. The federal court has a strong interest in keeping the federal issues in all cases decided correctly. So if the state court has decided a federal issue incorrectly, then you are likely to get a more objective and fair review of your case in federal court.

The federal courts must follow the decisions of the United States Supreme Court, the regional Court of Appeals (in California, this is the Ninth Circuit Court of Appeals), and the federal district court where the petition is filed. Cases decided by other federal courts can be persuasive, but are not binding law.

<u>Fourth Amendment Exception</u>

There is one important exception to the general rule that prisoners can bring federal habeas claims on any federal constitutional grounds. Violations of the U.S. Constitution's Fourth Amendment right to be free from unreasonable search and seizure may not be challenged in a federal habeas corpus petition provided that there has been a full and fair review of the issue by the state courts. But again, as explained above, if you feel that your attorney did not properly raise the Fourth Amendment issue in your case, then you may be able to bring a habeas petition for a Sixth Amendment claim of ineffective assistance of counsel.

CRITICAL TIP: In order to preserve your ability to continue fighting your case in federal court through a petition for writ of habeas corpus, make sure to cite to federal law and the United States Constitution throughout your state appellate briefs. If you do not cite to federal law and thoroughly argue the federal issue, then you could be precluded from relief in federal court. In other words, make the state courts decide the federal issues.

2. ARGUING FEDERAL LAW IN YOUR STATE APPELLATE PROCEEDINGS

In order to preserve your ability to continue fighting your case in federal court through a petition for writ of habeas corpus, make sure to cite to federal law and the United States Constitution throughout your state appellate briefs. If you do not cite to federal law and thoroughly argue the federal issue, then you could be precluded from relief in federal court. In other words, make the state courts decide the federal issues.

For example, if you are going to argue that you were not properly informed of the plea agreement by your attorney and rejected the plea agreement due to the incompetence of your lawyer, there will be a state law that covers this issue. In Arizona, that law would be *State v. Donald*. If the Arizona inmate files an appellate brief arguing only *State v. Donald*, then the state court did not consider the ineffective assistance of counsel issue of under federal law, i.e., *U.S. v. Strickland*.

You will want to cite to both state law and federal law, but make sure to develop your federal law argument. It is not enough to simply cite to a federal case and preserve your right to go to federal court. You have to give the state courts the opportunity to evaluate, consider and decide the federal issue completely. A mere citation is insufficient for the federal courts to legitimately determine that the state court had an opportunity to decide the federal issues.

D. STANDARD OF REVIEW UNDER THE ANTI-TERRORISM EFFECTIVE DEATH PENALTY ACT (AEDPA)

It is critical to your petition's success that you understand the standard of review that the federal courts will use to evaluate your claims. That standard of review is found in the Antiterrorism and Effective Death Penalty Act of 1996 ("AEDPA"). Congress passed AEDPA in response to complaints that prisoners were abusing the writ of habeas corpus by them filing multiple petitions challenging their convictions on frivolous grounds, often years after their convictions became final. This is where the statute of limitations was born, along with other limitations.

One of those limitations is the standard of review that will be used to evaluate your claims in your federal habeas corpus petition. If you are at the stage of your case where you are considering federal court, then you have already challenged your conviction and sentence in state court. You filed all available appeals and petitions for review with the state appellate courts. If done properly, those state appellate courts have considered and decided issues relating to your federal issues. Here is where the standards come in to play.

When the federal court reviews the petition, it has limited power to overturn the state court decisions in the case. A federal court may not grant a petition for writ of habeas corpus on any claim that has been decided on the merits in state court. There are two areas where an inmate can attack the state courts' decision in federal court. The standards are that (1) the state court decision was contrary to, or involved an unreasonable application of, clearly established federal law, or (2) the state court decision was based on an unreasonable determination of the facts in light of the evidence presented in the state court proceeding. Both of these areas of attack will be explained below.

1. Contrary to, or Unreasonable Application of Federal Law

Again, the federal court will not grant you any relief on any claim that was decided on the merits in state court. That statement sounds as though if the state court decides an issue, then you cannot raise it in federal court. That is not true.

What you have to do is determine which area of attack (or both) that your case falls under. Ask yourself, "Was the state courts' decision contrary to or an unreasonable application of clearly established federal law?" If the answer is "yes," then you have a valid claim under 28 U.S.C. Sec. 2254 and you should file the petition for writ of habeas corpus.

So what does "contrary to or unreasonable application of federal law" mean?

<u>Contrary To</u>

A state court's decision "is contrary to ...clearly established federal law",..."if the state court applies a rule that contradicts the governing law set forth" in a controlling Supreme Court case, or "if the state court confronts facts that are materially indistinguishable from a relevant Supreme Court precedent and arrives at a result opposite" to the holding. *Williams v. Taylor*, 529 U.S. 362, 405, 412-413 (2000) (Justice O'Connor).

So if you are arguing your claims under the "contrary to" standard, then you need to find a U.S. Supreme Court case to argue throughout your state court appellate proceedings. You should then evaluate the facts of your case with that U.S. Supreme Court case, as well as the legal reasoning the U.S. Supreme Court used to reach the conclusions it did when deciding that case. Now, you would compare how the state appellate courts evaluated your case as it relates to the controlling U.S. Supreme Court case. If the state courts decided your case differently, even though the facts or issues are the same, then you would have a strong argument under the "contrary to" standard.

Unreasonable Application Of

As for "unreasonable application", a federal court may grant relief "if the state court identifies the correct governing legal principle from [the Supreme Court's] decisions but unreasonably applies that principle to the facts of the petitioner's case." Id.;. *Ramdass v. Angelone*, 530 U.S.156 (2000).

When a claim falls under the "unreasonable application" clause, the state court's application of the Supreme Court precedent must be "objectively unreasonable," not just incorrect. *Wiggins v. Smith*, 539 U.S. 510, 520-21 (2003).

Under *Williams v. Taylor*, 529 U.S. 420 (2000), the emphasis of the federal court's inquiry is on the nature and quality of the state court decision.

E. Motion for Appointment of Counsel

While the Rules Governing Section 2254 Cases in the U.S. District Courts mention the appointment of counsel only with regard to discovery and evidentiary hearings, the CJA in 18 U.S.C. § 3006A(a)(2)(B) permits discretionary appointment at any stage of the proceedings in the interest of justice.

Specifically, 18 U.S.C. § 3006A(a)(2)(B) states, "Each United States district court, with the approval of the judicial council of the circuit, shall place in operation throughout the district a plan for furnishing representation for any person financially unable to obtain adequate representation in accordance with this section. Representation under each plan shall include counsel and investigative, expert, and other services necessary for adequate representation. Each plan shall provide the following: Whenever the United States magistrate judge or the court determines that the interests of justice so require, representation may be provided for any financially eligible person who ... is seeking relief under section 2241, **2254,** or 2255 of title 28." 18 U.S.C. § 3006A(a)(2)(B).

After your state court proceedings have finished and you are ready to proceed to federal district court with your federal habeas corpus petition, you should file a motion for appointment of counsel with the district court. **(See, Form #1 – Motion for Appointment of Counsel).**

F. Obtaining The Record, Transcripts and Trial File

Your post-conviction and/or appellate lawyer is responsible for sending the file to you. Exactly what makes up "the file" varies with each attorney and each case. At a minimum, you need to obtain copies (or originals) of the transcripts in your case, the file the trial attorney used (even if you accepted a plea agreement it's called "the trial file") and the documents that were filed with the court. If you had an appeal, the documents that were filed with the clerk of the court are collected and put into what's called a Record on Appeal. If you accepted a plea agreement, you'll have to collect your own record, which should consist of the documents filed by the prosecutor and your lawyer with the clerk of the court. The attorney who was assigned to represent you with respect to your post-conviction should send you those records.

1. Your Right To Prepare

You will be held to a high standard when it comes to how your petition for writ of habeas corpus is prepared and, potentially, your appeal to the circuit court of appeals. As a part of that standard, you will be expected to file with your petition any and all documents that support your claims. If you fail to support your claims with the evidence that was used in the trial court, then in all likelihood, the federal court will not favorably review your petition.

The nature of federal habeas corpus is that the federal court is being asked to review what the state court reviewed when making the decisions in your case. You are essentially telling the federal court that the state court incorrectly decided the federal law issues in your case based on the evidence that was presented to the state court. The federal court will want to see that evidence when making its decision.

Because you are going to be held to a high standard when filing your petition, you have the right to review the necessary documents to support your claims. When requesting documents from the lawyer who handled your state case, make sure to be specific as to which documents you need and why you need them. Do not simply list a large number of documents and demand them. I have known attorneys who have received those lists and filed a notice with the court asking which documents are to be supplied to the defendant. There is a good chance the judge will order that you only get a limited number of the documents you requested.

CRITICAL TIP: The better practice is to be respectful and pleasant with your state court lawyer when asking for documents. It would also be wise to break up your requests for any large list of documents. Having said that, if you are requesting either the transcripts and/or the record on appeal, you have the right to those documents, so you can be more demanding. Just remember, you may have to ask this same lawyer for a favor later on. If you've been rude or demanding to him or her, chances are you won't get the favor granted.

If you are not having good communication with your attorney via letters, then ask your counselor at the prison to set up a legal call with your attorney so you can speak to him or her over the phone. Sometimes talking with the attorney can help smooth things over if communication has been shaky. In addition, often what one person writes in a letter is misinterpreted by the person reading the letter. Speaking to one another will clarify things.

2. TRIAL ATTORNEY, APPELLATE ATTORNEY, POST-CONVICTION ATTORNEY—WHO IS SUPPOSED TO SEND YOU WHAT, EXACTLY

Let's break it down a little further as to who is supposed to send you what materials:

Trial Attorney
Again, this person is the lawyer you went to trial with and/or accepted a plea agreement with. The trial attorney should not have to send you any documents. The reason for that is because your post-conviction attorney should have requested and received the trial file from the trial attorney. The only way the trial attorney should have the trial file is if the post-conviction attorney sent the trial file back to the trial attorney, which would be odd because your post-conviction attorney should know that he or she is required to pass along that file to you.

If you receive the trial file (from either the trial attorney or post-conviction attorney) and there are documents missing or other documents from the file you need, then you should request those documents first from the trial attorney. Get that person to say that they do not have the requested document and then request it from your post-conviction attorney. If the document is not with the trial attorney, then it should be with the post-conviction attorney.

Post-Conviction Attorney
The majority of your materials will come from your post-conviction attorney. The post-conviction attorney is responsible for collecting the materials that are needed to properly review your case. Typically, those materials include the trial file (with police reports, attorney notes (those are <u>not confidential</u> if you're alleging ineffective assistance of counsel), all disclosure from the State, pleadings that were filed and correspondence (letters and emails) regarding your case), the appellate record (if you had a trial) and the transcripts.

Be sure to contact the attorney if you have not received the materials within a reasonable time. And if you do not get a response from the attorney within ten (10) days, then write a letter to the judge indicating that you have not received the materials. It is important to keep a written record of your activities on the case so that if it becomes an issue later you won't have to rely upon your memory. In addition, issues often arise where it will be your word against another person's word—make sure your word is written down (and preferably filed with the court).

Appellate Attorney
If you had a trial, then you more than likely had an appeal. If your appeal is completed and the court of appeals issued a ruling, then your appellate attorney should have sent to you the record on appeal and the transcripts of the trial and sentencing. Even though your appellate attorney has sent the transcripts and record on appeal to you, you may receive a second copy from your post-conviction attorney. Again, the record on appeal consists of all

pleadings that were filed in your case, minute entries, the jury instructions, and any exhibits that were admitted at trial.

Between your trial attorney, post-conviction attorney and your appellate attorney, you should receive all of the materials you need to properly prepare your pro per petition for post-conviction relief.

CRITICAL TIP: In order to know that you have received everything that was filed with the court and, therefore, you have a complete file, you should request a "docket sheet" from your attorney, or if the attorney will not provide one, then from the clerk of the court where you had your trial or accepted a plea agreement. The docket sheet shows everything that has been filed with the clerk of the court in your case. You can cross-reference the materials you have received with the docket sheet to ensure you have everything in your case.

G. How To Obtain Other Documents, Exhibits And Witnesses

Often times, even after receiving all of the materials from your attorneys you will need more documents, videos, records and/or statements from people. You must request leave from the court, or permission from the court, to conduct discovery (obtain more evidence in your case).

A judge may, for good cause, authorize a party to conduct discovery under the Federal Rules of Civil Procedure and may limit the extent of discovery. If necessary for effective discovery, the judge must appoint an attorney for a petitioner who qualifies to have counsel appointed under 18 U.S.C. § 3006A.

A party requesting discovery must provide reasons for the request. The request must also include any proposed interrogatories and requests for admission, and must specify any requested documents.

If you are seeking to compel disclosure from the prosecutor (or any other party who does not comply with your court-approved discovery requests), then you will need the court's assistance to do so. You can file a motion to compel with the trial court and ask that the court issue an order requiring the party to provide you with the materials you have requested from them.

If the judge grants your motion to compel, the court will issue an order for you to receive the materials. If you still do not receive the materials, then you'll want to request a hearing where the party will be forced to come to court and explain why they are not providing you with the materials.

3. Drafting the Petition for a Writ of Habeas Corpus

Drafting the petition for habeas corpus is going to be one of the most difficult parts of your case. Everything up until now has been preparing you to write the petition. Writing an effective petition is your only opportunity to convince a judge to grant you the relief that you request. The sections below will instruct you how to not only properly prepare your petition, but also how to write effectively and persuasively when preparing the petition in order to give you the best chance of success.

A. Outline, Organize, Then Organize Again

Organization is the key to success. Write that down and put it up on your wall. Remember it. That's how you will succeed in this and every other project you take on. This point can't be stressed enough. In order to have a successful petition, or any other motion you draft, the organization will be the key to that success. If you have a well-organized petition, then it will be easier for the reader (in your case, the judge) to understand your arguments and follow them to a logical conclusion, which is the relief you are asking them for. If they can't follow your arguments, then you lower your chances of success.

With respect to writing your petition, the first part of that organization will be to draft an outline of what your petition will look like.

When you have an outline of your petition, it will be much easier to write the petition. You will be able to see (literally) where your petition is headed and which sections you need to focus on. You can also adjust arguments based on how your outline flows and make sure to keep the petition nicely structured. Most importantly, your arguments will be clear and well thought out when you create an outline.

Once you feel like you have created a solid outline, spend a day or two away from the outline, not thinking about it. Afterwards, come back to it and re-read it and see if the arguments still flow nicely and make sense in the order you created them. If so, you have a final outline to work off of. If not, re-organize the outline and edit any parts that don't flow with the way you set up the arguments. Remember, make it as easy as possible for the reader to understand your arguments.

B. Standard Form Petition vs. Using Pleading Paper

Each district court in the United States has a standardized form on their website for filing a petition for a writ of habeas corpus. These forms are fill-in-the-blank forms. The forms vary slightly from district to district. The forms are typically easy to follow, asking you to fill in standard information about your case, your convictions, sentences and attorneys who represented you during your trial court and appellate cases. The forms also ask you to list the grounds you feel warrant relief in your case. These forms do not encourage you to analyze those grounds, only to list the grounds a small section (a few lines) for providing factual support.

If you do not wish to use the form, then you can prepare your petition for a writ of habeas corpus using pleading paper, as explained below. If you use pleading paper to file your petition, then you are able to expand on your arguments and cite to your record and the law that supports your claims.

CRITICAL TIP: If you use pleading paper to prepare your petition for a writ of habeas corpus, then it is essential that you include each section that is listed below and is listed on the standard form in your district. The pleading that you file must conform to the standard form in your district.

C. Standard Form Petition

The benefit to using a standard form to file your petition for a writ of habeas corpus is that you are using a form that the court you are filing in uses routinely and knows well. The form asks you specific questions and the answers to those questions are readily available to you if you have a copy of your file. In other words, it's much easier to file a petition using the standard form rather than writing it out on pleading paper.

The downside to using the standard form is that you do not control what information the court reviews when it reviews your petition. The standard form encourages you to be brief with the grounds you feel warrant relief and limit your ability to argue your side of the case.

It will be for you to decide which strategy you use in filing your petition. For whichever strategy you use, it is essential that you are thorough in preparing the petition. The following sections are designed to help you fill out the standard form petition.

1. Caption Page

At the top of each standard form will be an area that has the following items listed for you to fill out: Name, Prisoner Number, Institutional Address.

Under the address section will be the court where you are filing your petition. You should be filing your petition in the district where you are in custody. The districts are usually described by "Northern District of," or "Eastern District of," whichever state you are in. It varies for each state so make sure to check which district you are in before filing, and use that district's standard form. But even if you happen to file in the wrong district, the district that you file in should transfer your petition to the correct district and then notify you of the transfer. Do not rely on them to transfer your case, however. Do a little research and find out which federal district you are in and which federal district court you should file your petition in.

Under the name of the federal district court will be where you name the Petitioner and the Respondent. You are the petitioner so you should write your name on the line that has "Petitioner" next to it. The Respondent is the name of the warden for your state. By filing a federal habeas corpus relating to your state conviction, you are essentially suing the warden of the state in a civil case, arguing that they have you in custody illegally. That's why you are the petitioner and the warden is the respondent.

2. Information About Your Conviction, Sentence and Proceedings

As explained above, these sections of the standard form petition are straightforward. You fill out the information being requested. For your conviction and sentence, you'll be focused on the very first court you were in when you were fighting your case. That would be the trial court, which is usually the "superior court." You will be required to provide the name of the court, the address of the court, your original case number (not an appellate case number), the date you were sentenced, the length of your prison sentence and the crimes you were sentenced for.

There should be additional, specific questions regarding your trial court proceedings, such as whether you had an arraignment, preliminary hearing, grand jury proceeding or if there were any pretrial motions filed in your case.

The questions will then focus on the outcome of your case, such as if you pled guilty or exercised your right to a jury trial. And if you went to trial, if the trial was before a judge or jury, and how many days the trial was. There will be questions regarding whether or not you appealed your case and, if so, to which courts.

CRITICAL TIP: Some of these questions seem harmless but they could get your petition dismissed quickly. For example, there is a standard question that is typically asked regarding whether you are raising new claims in the federal district court that were not raised in the trial court. This question is focus on the exhaustion requirement. Your petition could be denied depending on your answer to this seemingly innocuous question.

For all of the proceedings above, the standard form will likely ask you to provide information about the attorney who represented you for each of those proceedings.

3. Grounds for Relief

In the standard form petition, you will be given a few lines to state what claim you have and the facts that support the claim. Typically, there will be space for three claims and it will be on one page. Again, like previously explained, the form petition encourages you to be brief.

If you are using a standard form petition, then you are permitted to attach additional pages to the form in order to expand on your grounds for relief. You can use the pleading paper provided with this Manual to expand your grounds of relief and attach to the form petition.

CRITICAL TIP: It is imperative that you include each and every ground for relief that you feel you have in the first petition for a writ of habeas corpus. If you leave out a ground for relief and attempt to raise it later in a subsequent petition, then it is likely that the federal district court will dismiss your petition without even considering the merits of the petition. See, *McCleskey v. Zant*, 499 U.S. 467, 111 S.Ct. 1454, 113 L.Ed.2d 517 (1991).

If you are using the standard form to draft your petition for a writ of habeas corpus then more than likely the form will encourage you to be brief when it comes to stating your grounds for relief. For example, the instructions in the standard form used in this Manual tells you to, "State briefly every reason why you believe you are being confined unlawfully."

You can't be too brief when it comes to drafting your grounds of relief, otherwise the court may find that you failed to properly develop your arguments. On the other hand, if you write arguments that are too wordy, the court is not likely to read everything you write.

In the sections below, the Manual explains how to write concise legal argument that are short enough to be read in their entirety, but also be effective with their goal. In any event, make sure to draft clear arguments that are supported by facts and law. While this Manual will go into much great detail later **(See, Section 3(E))**, a good way to structure your argument is to identify the specific issue you are addressing in a particular ground, tell the court what the controlling law is on that specific issue, discuss the specific facts of your case and how those facts warrant relief based on the law you discussed, and then be clear as to what relief you want based on your analysis.

Again, this Manual goes into much greater detail as to how to write your legal arguments in later sections. So whether you are using the standard form to draft your petition, or are using pleading paper, make sure to structure your arguments in a clear, concise and effective manner.

4. Timeliness of the Petition

Some standard forms from certain districts have a specific section to address the timeliness of your petition. Timeliness of petitions for writs of habeas corpus was covered in Section 2(B) of this Manual so review that section before filling out the timeliness section of a standard form.

When filling out the timeliness section of the standard form, make sure to remember the tolling periods that would apply to you, the time that you had to file a brief with the U.S. Supreme Court and any other tolling circumstances that would apply to you.

D. USING PLEADING PAPER

If you choose to prepare your petition for writ of habeas corpus by using pleading paper rather than the standard form provided by the district court, then you will need to make sure each of the sections below are addressed in your petition. The majority of the following sections are basic information about your case, but they are necessary and need to be included in the petition. If you fail to include any of these sections, then you risk the court dismissing your petition.

Attached to this Manual is a sample petition for a writ of habeas corpus that was filed in a case that received an oral argument in the U.S. Court of Appeals for the Ninth Circuit. **(See, Form #2 – Sample Petition for a Writ of Habeas Corpus)**

1. CAPTION

The caption page is simply the first page of your petition for post-conviction relief or any other pleading you file with the court. A pleading is simply a legal document, usually consisting of the numbers 1-28 along the left-hand side of the page. You don't have to have pleading paper to file the petition (I have provided you with 10 pages of blank pleading paper if you want to use it.)

The caption page will have your contact information in the top-left hand corner of the page. Underneath your contact information, centered in the middle of the page, you will write which court you are filing the pleading in. Underneath the court name and to the left side of the document, you will write the Petitioner vs. Respondent section. The Respondent in a 2254 federal habeas corpus case is the name of the director or secretary of prisons of the state in which you are being held in custody. You are the Petitioner; hence you are filing a petition. In your state case, you were used to seeing, "State of Arizona v." or "The People of California v." as the plaintiff. In a 2254 case, it's you versus the warden who is holding your body.

By filing a federal habeas corpus relating to your state conviction, you are essentially suing the person who runs and operates the prison system of the state in a civil case, arguing that they have you in custody illegally. That's why you are the petitioner and the director or secretary of the prison is the respondent.

The term, "writ of habeas corpus," means to "produce the body." What you are asking for in the petition is for the judge to produce your body before the court so that the judge can make a determination as to whether the director or secretary is detaining your body for a valid reason. Your petition will describe why your conviction is not valid, and therefore, why the director or secretary should be ordered to free your body.

Directly opposite of the "Plaintiff v. Defendant" language there will be three items written down: 1) your case number(s) if you have them for your federal habeas corpus case (leave this blank if you don't have a case number and the clerk will fill one in), 2) the name of the document (Motion to..., or, Petition for Writ of Habeas Corpus), and 3) the judge's name your case is assigned to (again, leave this blank if you don't know the judge's name yet). That will complete the caption part of the pleading.

2. PARTIES

As explained in the "Caption" section above, you are the petitioner in a petition for a writ of habeas corpus proceeding. You are petitioning the district court for specific relief, so you are the petitioner.

The respondent is the director or secretary of the prison system in the state you are in and controls the prison in which you are being held. Who that person is should be readily available to you in the prison, or you can ask one of your counselors who that person is and then list them as the respondent.

You also want to find out who represents the director or secretary of prisons in habeas corpus proceedings. Typically, that will be the state attorney general in your state. Currently, Rob Bonta is the attorney general for California, and Mark Brnovich is the attorney general for Arizona. If you are filing a habeas petition in either California or Arizona, either Bonta or Brnovich would be the person you identify as a party to the case.

3. JURISDICTION

The next two sections are jurisdiction and venue. These are similar concepts because the two concepts decide where (which court) you bring your case.

Jurisdiction answers the question of whether *any* federal district court is able to hear your case. In other words, do you have the right to bring your case to federal court?

The controlling jurisdictional federal statute is 28 U.S.C. § 1331. That statute reads, "The district courts shall have original jurisdiction of all civil actions arising under the Constitution, laws, or treaties of the United States." This statute is telling you that as long as you have a federal issue to raise involving the U.S. Constitution or any other federal law, then your case if properly before a federal district court. If you only had issues involving state laws to raise, then your case would not be proper in federal district court.

For this section, an argument is not needed as to what those federal laws are, only that you have issues under the U.S. Constitution or other federal laws. For example, the following sentences should suffice for showing jurisdiction is proper before a federal district court: "The United States District Court has jurisdiction over the petition for a writ of habeas corpus pursuant to 28 U.S.C. § 2254 and 1331. Petitioner is in custody pursuant to a judgment of an Arizona state court and seeks relief on the ground that his imprisonment and sentence are in violation of his rights under the United States Constitution."

4. VENUE

Now that you have established that the federal district court has jurisdiction because you have federal claims to raise, you have to pinpoint which federal district court is the correct one to bring your case.

There are ninety-four (94) federal district courts in the United States. Each state has at least one federal district court. If you do not know which federal district court is the one where venue is proper for you, then, if you have access to the internet, you can search for the proper court by going to uscourts.gov/federal-court-finder/search. That website will allow you to input your address or zip code and then will list the federal district court where you should file your case, along with every other federal entity that involves the court system, including the federal public defender and the U.S. Court of Appeal that you may end up filing in if your habeas petition is unsuccessful.

The federal statute controlling venue is 28 U.S.C. § 2241(d):

"Where an application for a writ of habeas corpus is made by a person in custody under the judgment and sentence of a State court of a State which contains two or more Federal judicial districts, the application may be filed in the district court for the district wherein such person is in custody or in the district court for the district within which the State court was held which convicted and sentenced him and each of such district courts shall have concurrent jurisdiction to entertain the application. The district court for the district wherein such an application is filed in the exercise of its discretion and in furtherance of justice may transfer the application to the other district court for hearing and determination."

The benefit of the venue statute is that it allows district courts to transfer a case to the correct venue if the case was filed in the incorrect venue. Do not rely on the district court's ability to do so, however, because it is not mandatory that the case be transferred if it is incorrectly filed. Often times petitioners are filing very close to the deadline to file their habeas petitions, so to file in the incorrect court could be detrimental.

5. PROCEDURAL HISTORY

The procedural history of your case is the main events that happened in your case in the trial court. You should indicate when and by whom you were indicted and for what charges, explain how you were found guilty of those charges (guilty plea or by a jury) and detail what your prison sentence is based on those convictions.

6. APPEALS

If you had an appeal in the state court system, then this is the section where you explain those proceedings. This can be a brief section where you simply indicate if you had an appeal, and what was the result of the appeal.

This section only applies to defendant who exercised their right to a trial and, therefore, had a right to an appeal. Typically, if you accept a plea agreement you give up your right to an appeal and can only collaterally attack your conviction through state post-conviction relief proceedings.

7. STATE POST-CONVICTION RELIEF PROCEEDINGS

This section applies to defendants who accepted a plea agreement, as well as those who exercised their right to a trial because both groups are permitted to challenge their convictions through state post-conviction relief proceedings.

In this section, highlight the main events that took place during your post-conviction relief proceedings: when it was filed, the result in the trial court, and then explain any appellate proceedings that occurred as a result of being denied post-conviction relief. These appellate proceedings are not from a direct appeal following a trial, these appellate proceedings occurred after you filed a post-conviction relief petition and was denied.

8. FEDERAL PROCEEDINGS

In this section explain any federal proceedings that have taken placed regarding the conviction(s) and sentences you are currently challenging in the federal habeas proceeding. Often times, there will be no federal proceedings because this will be the first time you are taking your case to federal court. In that case, you simply write one sentence that explains that this is the first federal petition for a writ of habeas corpus challenging your conviction.

9. PENDING PROCEEDINGS

Normally, this section would indicate that there are no current pending proceedings in state court. That's because in order to properly bring your case to federal court, your state court proceedings should have ended.

10. Representations

In this section, you write out all of the lawyers who represented you during your state court proceedings and for each proceeding (pre-trial, trial, appeal, post-conviction proceedings, etc.). You do not have to provide the attorney's contact information.

11. Other Prison Sentences

If you are serving any other prison sentences that you are not challenging in this petition for a writ of habeas corpus, then you explain what those sentences are in this section. List the court, case number, conviction and prison sentence.

12. Grounds for Relief

This section is not the section where you write out your arguments; that will come later. In this section, you identify the main issues that you will be addressing in your full argument, along with a citation to the controlling case or statute. Think of this section as your "elevator pitch." An elevator pitch is what you would say to someone about your case in the time you had to ride in an elevator with that person. Keep it brief, to the point and don't make it a discussion.

The first line of this section should be something similar to, "The grounds on which Petitioner contends his conviction are contrary to the Constitution of the United States are fully discussed in the attached Memorandum of Points and Authorities, which is incorporated herein." With this line, you are letting the judge know that you have a complete argument detailed about the grounds you are about to list later in the pleading.

13. Exhaustion

The exhaustion section is where you avow that you pursued your case in state court sufficiently enough that you are allowed to now bring the case to federal court. The avowal will look something similar to: "All grounds for relief raised in this petition for writ of habeas corpus have previously been presented to the Arizona Court of Appeals. Petitioner has not previously filed any type of petition, application or motion in a federal court regarding the conviction that Petitioner is challenging in this petition."

The statute controlling the exhaustion requirement is 28 U.S.C. § 2254(b)(1)(A): "An application for a writ of habeas corpus on behalf of a person in custody pursuant to the judgment of a State court shall not be granted unless it appears that—

> (A)the applicant has exhausted the remedies available in the courts of the State;

or

(B)(i)there is an absence of available State corrective process; or

(ii)circumstances exist that render such process ineffective to protect the rights of the applicant."

[For a full explanation of the exhaustion requirement, see Section 2(B)(2)]

14. Timeliness

The statute that controls the timeline to file a petition for a writ of habeas corpus in federal court is 28 U.S.C. § 2244 (d)(1), "A 1-year period of limitation shall apply to an application for a writ of habeas corpus by a person in custody pursuant to the judgment of a State court. The limitation period shall run from the latest of—

(A) the date on which the judgment became final by the conclusion of direct review or the expiration of the time for seeking such review;

(B) the date on which the impediment to filing an application created by State action in violation of the Constitution or laws of the United States is removed, if the applicant was prevented from filing by such State action;

(C) the date on which the constitutional right asserted was initially recognized by the Supreme Court, if the right has been newly recognized by the Supreme Court and made retroactively applicable to cases on collateral review; or

(D) the date on which the factual predicate of the claim or claims presented could have been discovered through the exercise of due diligence."

The most commonly-used starting date is Subsection (A): "the date on which the judgment became final by the conclusion of direct review or the expiration of the time for seeking such review." If no direct appeal was filed, the one-year statute of limitation begins running usually after a period of time following the judgment of conviction was entered.

If a direct appeal was filed and pursued through the state court system, the one-year statute of limitation does not start until expiration of the additional 90-day period "within which [a petitioner] could have filed a petition for a writ of certiorari from the United States Supreme Court" following direct appeal, whether or not one was filed. *Bowen v. Roe*, 188 F.3d 1157, 1159 (9th Cir.1999).

CRITICAL TIP: Please note that the additional 90-day certiorari period, however, does not apply to post-conviction relief actions, and so do not count that time period into your federal statute of limitations calculation.

[For a detailed examination on the timeliness issue for your petition, see Section 2(B)]

In this section, you will explain that your petition should not be barred because you filed your state-court appellate proceedings and pursued those according to state law, therefore the time spent pursing those claims in state court should be tolled (not counted) when it comes to the one-year deadline to file the petition for a writ of habeas corpus.

The tolling statute is 28 U.S.C. § 2244 (d)(2): "The time during which a properly filed application for State post-conviction or other collateral review with respect to the pertinent judgment or claim is pending shall not be counted toward any period of limitation under this subsection."

You then provide the date that the last state appellate court denied your appeal and then calculate the date your petition in federal court is due. You can calculate your due date using the information in this Manual, including the tolling and equitable tolling sections.

15. RELIEF REQUESTED

This is where you tell the court what you want it to do based on your arguments. You should be specific with your requests, but they normally include the following: 1) Ask the court to issue the writ (order) to have you brought to court; 2) require the respondent to provide the entire court record to the district court; 3) require the respondent to file an answer to your petition; 4) allow you to conduct discovery and expand the record accordingly; 5) conduct an evidentiary hearing on your claims; 6) ask for leave to brief any other issues that the district court may want briefed.

16. VERIFICATION

The verification section of the petition for a writ of habeas corpus is the section where you sign the petition under penalty of perjury that everything you have included in the petition is true and correct. Make sure to sign and date the petition.

17. POINTS AND AUTHORITIES

The points and authorities section is where you will now write out detailed arguments for all of the issues/grounds you wish to raise in your petition. As we discussed earlier, it is imperative that you keep your arguments organized so that the reader will be able to follow your arguments and provide you the relief you requested. The beginning of that organization is a table of contents for the remaining portion of your petition, the Memorandum of Points and Authorities.

The table of contents should be a roadmap of how your arguments will be laid out over the remainder of the brief. You should list the section you will be addressing and the page number where the reader can find that section.

The typical sections in a table of contents are as follows:

Procedural History and Statement of Relevant Facts
Jurisdictional Requirements
Exhaustion
Claims for Relief
Request for Evidentiary Hearing
Conclusion
Relief Requested

Often times, you are working on your legal arguments at the same time you are putting together the table of contents. You should plan out the arguments that you will raise, and then start to list them in the "Claims for Relief" section of the table of contents. You should only use one or two sentences in the "Claims for Relief" section to describe what your claim is. And each claim should be separated out as individual claims, not a paragraph of all claims together.

Now that you have the arguments you want to raise to the court, the next step is preparing those arguments. In the next sections, the Manual will help you develop those arguments in a way that will put you in the best position to get the relief you are requesting from the federal district court.

E. Drafting Persuasive Legal Arguments

In your petition for writ of habeas corpus, whether you use the form provided by the court in your district or you write it out yourself on pleading paper, you will need to draft your legal arguments. Over the years, I have worked with hundreds of pro per litigants. During that time, I have seen a wide spectrum of legal writing from those litigants, ranging from an unorganized letter that appears to be rambling, to neatly written, well thought out, concise legal arguments that are supported by relevant facts. The main purpose of this Manual is to get you to the end of the spectrum that has you drafting sound legal arguments that will get you the relief you are seeking in court.

1. Caption Page

The caption page is simply the first page of your petition for post-conviction relief or any other pleading you file with the court. A pleading is simply a legal document, usually consisting of the numbers 1-28 along the left-hand side of the page. You don't have to have pleading paper to file the petition (I have provided you with 10 pages of blank pleading paper if you want to use it.)

The caption page will have your contact information in the top-left hand corner of the page. Underneath your contact information, centered in the middle of the page, you will write which court you are filing the pleading in. Underneath the court name and to the left side of the document, you will write the Plaintiff v. Defendant section. The Defendant in a 2254 federal habeas corpus case is the name of the warden of the state in which you are being held in custody. You are the Plaintiff. In your state case, you were used to seeing, "State of Arizona v." or "The People of California v." as the plaintiff. By filing a federal habeas corpus relating to your state conviction, you are essentially suing the warden of the state in a civil case, arguing that they have you in custody illegally. That's why you are the plaintiff and the warden is the defendant.

Directly opposite of the "Plaintiff v. Defendant" language there will be three items written down: 1) your case number(s) if you have them for your federal habeas corpus case (leave this blank if you don't have a case number and the clerk will fill one in), 2) the name of the document (Motion to..., or, Petition for Writ of Habeas Corpus), and 3) the judge's name your case is assigned to (again, leave this blank if you don't know the judge's name yet). That will complete the caption part of the pleading. Anything written after that is the body of the pleading/petition.

2. Procedural History and Statement Of Relevant Facts

"Facts are stubborn things." –John Adams, representing English soldiers following the Boston Massacre.

In this section, you will weave together the procedural history of your case along with the statement of facts that happened in your case. Previously, you were instructed to give an "elevator pitch" when indicating what your claims of relief are earlier in the petition. This section is the opposite of the elevator pitch; this is the sit-down, telling a compelling story version. But even though you are telling the story of your case, keep it as concise as possible.

The statement of facts is extremely important to drafting a successful petition for a writ of habeas corpus. The arguments you make throughout your brief will hinge on the facts that you put into the statement of facts.

One of the first parts of the petition many judges flip to is the statement of facts. In order to have an effective statement of facts, you have to be objective with the facts. That means admitting or conceding certain aspects of your case and focusing on the strong points of your case. Judges, and their law clerks (who often read the petitions prior to the judge even reading them), appreciate it when the statement of facts is objective and not used as an argument—you can do that later in the petition.

CRITICAL TIP: You don't want to leave out a fact or facts just because they are not in your favor. If you do this, and the State puts the damaging facts in their brief, then you will lose credibility. Often times, if you leave out damaging facts, the State will not only mention the damaging facts, but will do everything it can to highlight those facts and the fact that you didn't mention them.

Citing to the Record

While writing your statement of facts, you should cite to the record. What that means is to tell the judge and prosecutor where you are getting your information.

For state appeals, the clerk of the court prepares what is called a Record on Appeal. The Record on Appeal, or ROA as it is referred to in briefs, contains all of the court filings by all parties in the case.

If you accepted a plea agreement and filed a petition for post-conviction relief and then were denied, you should have appealed that denial to the court of appeals in your state. That appeal would then create a record on appeal. That would be the record that you cite to when you are preparing your petition.

CRITICAL TIP: To help you easily cite to the record on appeal, you can ask the clerk of the court or your attorney for a docket sheet. The docket sheet will list all of the documents that were filed as part of your record on appeal.

The way to cite to the record in your petition is to write the sentence that you want and in that sentence you will refer to a minute order, pleading, or other document that was filed in court. Each page of the record on appeal is numbered; it's called Bates stamped. If you cite to a document that is Bates stamped 005 to 016, then you would write your sentence and then put, "ROA 005-016" after the sentence. For example, if you refer to your indictment it would read, "The state caused an indictment to be issued on May 5, 2021. ROA 007-009." The ROA 007-009 would be the Bates stamped pages of the indictment. The Bates stamped numbers are typically on the lower right or middle of each page.

If you were citing to a court reporter's transcript of a hearing, then you would use the letters, "R.T." to indicate that you are referring to a transcript of a hearing. Following the "R.T.," you would list the date of the hearing, and after the date you would list the page number(s). So the citation would look like, "R.T., 10/15/2021, pp. 5-7."

Relevant Facts

Often times defendants want to write out each and every fact that occurred during their case. The statement of facts becomes incredibly long and you lose the reader quickly. The better practice is to only write the facts that are relevant to your argument.

For example, if you are raising an issue about your sentencing and how the judge sentenced you under the incorrect statute, the facts of the crime are irrelevant. What the judge is going to need to know is the crime you were found guilty of (including the statute) and the statute you were sentenced under. The specific details of the crime would be irrelevant, for the most part, in that analysis. Therefore, they aren't needed in the petition.

It's difficult for most attorneys and pro se litigants to only include the relevant facts. Most of the time, people want to reargue their case through the statement of facts. Resist the temptation to reargue your case—you'll have a chance to argue your case later in the petition.

Now that you know to only include the relevant facts, the second trick is to keep it concise (i.e., short). Get to the point. If you're sticking only to the relevant facts, chances are your statement of facts will be concise.

3. RELEVANT AND CONCISE LAW

If you're reading this, then more than likely you're in prison. One of the hardest things to find in prison is relevant case law, rules and statutes. It's almost impossible for an inmate to cite up-to-date case law—most lawyers don't even cite up-to-date case law.

Having said that, it is important for you to cite relevant case law. And this isn't the case law that you get from legal beagles on the yard that use the same case law for each and every petition. Relevant case law is case law that goes to the heart of your issue. Relevant case law is not general "due process" or "violation of rights" case law—that's going to apply to every claim that is made, generally.

You need to cite case law that addresses the exact issue you are arguing. So if you are arguing that the jury didn't find an aggravating factor that is also part of the element of the offense, find a case that addresses that issue.

How do you find that case? The best practice is to write to your previous counsel and explain what your exact issue is and then ask if they could send you a case or two that covers that issue. With a specific request, your previous counsel should send you a couple of cases.

Also, this Manual provides you with annotated cases that relate to petitions for writs of habeas corpus. You can use those cases in order to support your petition.

4. WHAT'S YOUR POINT? (ANALYSIS OF HOW YOUR FACTS FIT THE LAW)

In law school, all students are taught the IRAC method of legal writing. The acronym stands for Issue, Rule, Analysis and Conclusion. You should utilize that method when writing your pro se petition arguments. So after you have drafted your statement of facts, you will begin your argument section called the Claims for Relief section. Within that section is where you will utilize the IRAC method.

Details on How to Use the IRAC Method

Drafting Your Issue

First, you identify the **issue** that you want address. When it comes to writing out the issue you are addressing, there is a correct way to write out your issue and an incorrect way. Let's assume that you are raising an issue relating to ineffective assistance of counsel. One way to identify that issue in your petition is to write the following statement: "Trial counsel provided ineffective assistance of counsel." That statement, however, is generic and does not tell the reader anything about your particular issue or what to expect when they read your argument.

The correct way to write an issue is as follows: "Trial counsel provided ineffective assistance of counsel by failing to find, interview, and call as a witness at trial the only eye-witness to the shooting which the State of Arizona charged Petitioner with second-degree murder for when that eye-witness's testimony would have supported Petitioner's claim of self-defense." With an issue statement like this one, the reader already has a good understanding of your argument. This statement piques the reader's interest and begs the question: If this statement is true, then shouldn't the petitioner get relief?

Explaining the Law that Controls Your Issue

After you identify the issue, then you'll explain the **rule** (or case law) that will control your issue. In most petitions, the case law will be regarding ineffective assistance of counsel. That law is contained in the sample petition provided with this manual. **(See, Form #2)**

CRITICAL TIP: If there are competing cases, explain those cases in your petition—acting like cases that hurt your position don't exist will do nothing to help your case. The prosecutor will be using any and all cases that contradict your position so the better practice is to get in front of the prosecutor by raising the contradicting case law and highlighting how that case is inapplicable to your case.

If you are not raising an ineffective assistance of counsel claim, make sure you cite relevant case law that corresponds to your issue. Again, do not cite generic "due process" law for your issue. Do what you can to cite to case law that discusses your specific issue.

Analyze How the Law Supports Your Issue

The third part of your argument will be the **analysis** portion. This is the meat of your petition and where you need to convince the judge that you are entitled to the relief you are seeking.

CRITICAL TIP: In the analysis portion of your argument you will write out the most important facts that support your issue. You need to tell the story of your case and then weave the law that you previously cited back into the argument that you are making with the facts you are using. While this section is the most important section of your petition, make sure to be concise—don't write too much because the reader will start to skim your argument instead of reading it as careful as you would want them to.

The analysis you do to draft your arguments starts with preparing an outline for each issue that you will be addressing in your petition. A good outline will have the issue at the top of the page. Underneath the issue you should put the major points of law that you need to address for that issue. That requires you to dissect the case law that controls your issue and pull out the main areas of law that you'll be addressing.

Once you have the areas of law identified on your page, then you should put the facts of your case that support the position you are taking and that align with the case law you have listed. When you write the facts of your case under the law that corresponds with those facts, you'll also want to write the facts of the case you are using that are similar to your facts. You will use the case's facts to show how your case is similar to the case and how your judge should come to the same conclusion as the case's judge because the facts are similar. Generically, it looks something like this: "X, Y & Z facts supported a finding of ineffective assistance of counsel in State v. Sample, and in my case X, Y & Z facts are also present, and as such, my attorney provided ineffective assistance of counsel."

An real example looks something like this: "Similar to the defendant in State v. Tyler requesting a new attorney prior to his trial because his attorney failed to contact him or provide him with any discovery, [your name] also requested a new attorney at the pre-trial hearing, the motion to suppress hearing, and the trial readiness conference due to [attorney's name] failing to make any meaningful contact with me and failing to provide me with any discovery." By doing this comparison, the reader will recognize how your case is similar to the case you cited.

CRITICAL TIP: The best practice is to prepare rough drafts of your arguments on separate pieces of paper. You'll want to draft your arguments with enough time where you can put them away for a couple of days and then come back to them and re-read them. That time away will clear your head and allow you to see your arguments with a fresh mind and you'll be able to sharpen your arguments. Prepare as many rough drafts as you can until you feel the final product is ready to be

prepared.

Concluding Your Argument

The final part of your petition will be the **conclusion**. While some think the conclusion is just an afterthought and not important—they are incorrect. Use the conclusion effectively—tell the judge exactly what you want. Don't just state, "Petitioner requests whatever relief is proper under the law," or something to that effect. Instead, tell the judge that you want findings of fact that the attorney provided ineffective assistance of counsel, or that you want to keep the plea agreement in tact but are requesting to be resentenced. Remember: keep in clear and concise, the judge will appreciate it. But most importantly, be specific about the exact relief you are seeking.

F. EVIDENTIARY HEARING

Many inmates ask, "When do I go back to court on my case?" when I first speak to them. They are wondering when they can get a court date with the judge to explain their arguments. Habeas corpus cases rarely go back into court. And when they do make it back into the courtroom, it is almost always for an evidentiary hearing.

Pursuant to 28 U.S.C. § 2254(e)(2), whether to hold an evidentiary hearing is a statutorily mandated determination. According to Section 2254(e)(2), the district court generally may hold an evidentiary hearing only when the petitioner has shown that either the claim relies on a new, retroactive rule of constitutional law that was previously unavailable (28 U.S.C. § 2254(e)(2)(A)(i)) or the claim relies on a factual basis that could not have been previously discovered through the exercise of due diligence (28 U.S.C. § 2254(e)(2)(A)(ii)); and the facts underlying the claim show by clear and convincing evidence that, but for the constitutional error, no reasonable jury would have convicted the petitioner (28 U.S.C. § 2254(e)(2)(B)).

The court uses evidentiary hearings to take testimony and receive evidence regarding the facts and issues raised in your petition—and only when the petition for post-conviction relief has put forth compelling and convincing arguments that show relief is more likely than not warranted.

CRITICAL TIP: If your petition for a writ of habeas corpus is granted and you are allowed to withdraw from your plea agreement or your granted a new trial, then you will be subject to a longer prison sentence. That doesn't mean you'll get a longer prison sentence, but it is a possibility. It is also a possibility that you will receive a shorter prison sentence. Of course the main goal is to get the case dismissed, but if you proceed with a petition for a writ of habeas corpus, you need to know that you are subjecting yourself to a potentially longer prison sentence.

1. Appointing Counsel For An Evidentiary Hearing

If the petition is not dismissed, the judge must review the answer, any transcripts and records of state-court proceedings, and any materials submitted under Rule 7 to determine whether an evidentiary hearing is warranted.

A judge may, under 28 U.S.C. § 636(b), refer the petition to a magistrate judge to conduct hearings and to file proposed findings of fact and recommendations for disposition.

If an evidentiary hearing is warranted, the judge must appoint an attorney to represent a petitioner who qualifies to have counsel appointed under 18 U.S.C. § 3006A. The judge must conduct the hearing as soon as practicable after giving the attorneys adequate time to investigate and prepare.

It is important you communicate with your attorney prior to the evidentiary hearing so that you two are on the same page with respect to the strategy you will be using at the hearing.

The judge will set the hearing out approximately 45 to 60 days, which will give you sufficient time to speak with your attorney and coordinate which evidence, witnesses, etc. will be presented at the hearing. If you rely solely upon your attorney to prepare for the hearing, then you have provided "ineffective assistance" to your attorney. No one cares about your case as much as you do—make sure to stay in contact with your attorney and know exactly what will be done (in terms of evidence and argument) at your evidentiary hearing.

You will still be at the prison when your evidentiary hearing is set and will be moved to the jail of the county where your hearing will take place. While at the prison, you should arrange legal calls with your attorney to begin the planning process for your evidentiary hearing. Once you are moved to the jail—which will be anywhere from a week to a couple of days before the hearing—then you can meet with your attorney face-to-face to finalize your strategy for the hearing.

CRITICAL TIP: Prior to being moved from the prison to the jail, you should copy and mail to your attorney all of the documents you want to use at the evidentiary hearing as exhibits. You should also bring a copy of those documents/exhibits with you when you are moved to the jail. Do not rely on your attorney and don't assume they will do certain tasks on your behalf; make sure to communicate often with them so you both know who is doing what and when.

You should also inform your attorney which witnesses you will want to call to testify at the evidentiary hearing and a list of questions you want asked of each witness.

2. WHAT HAPPENS AT THE HEARING

Now that you are prepared, have a strategy, your exhibits and argument ready, it's time to conduct the hearing. An evidentiary hearing is conducted similar to a criminal trial, except that you may be called to testify. In a criminal trial, a defendant does not have to testify, but in habeas corpus hearings, you can be called by the State to testify.

The format of the evidentiary hearing is as follows: the parties give opening statements, the defendant calls witnesses, the State calls witnesses, the defendant may call rebuttal witnesses (witnesses who rebut or disprove what the State's witnesses testified to) and then the parties give closing arguments. After the hearing, the judge will typically take the matter "under advisement," which means that he or she will issue a written decision at a later date.

3. ADDRESSING THE COURT

When speaking in court make sure to show respect for the court by addressing the judge as "your honor" or "judge," never by their name. Every word you say will be recorded by a court reporter or digital recording device so be sure to speak loudly and clearly. When referring to the prosecutor, you can call them by their last name, "Mr. or Mrs. X," or simply call them "the State."

4. GETTING WITNESSES TO COURT

Once an evidentiary hearing is set, you will have subpoena power during your proceedings. With respect to the evidentiary hearing, you should subpoena each witness you intend to call at the hearing.

CRITICAL TIP: If you do not subpoena the witnesses, then they may not show up. Subpoenaing the witnesses makes it binding on the witness that they show up for the hearing or else they will be violating a court order (the subpoena) and the court can issue sanctions against that person. Without a subpoena, you are just hoping the witness shows up.

Your attorney should subpoena witnesses on your behalf. Make sure to communicate frequently (in writing) with your attorney about which witnesses will be subpoenaed and ask for proof that the witnesses were served with a subpoena.

5. ASKING WITNESSES QUESTIONS

Because you will likely be appointed an attorney for your evidentiary hearing, you probably won't have to worry about questioning witnesses. But in the off chance that you are required to ask witnesses questions, here is an explanation of how to effective examine witnesses on the witness stand.

There are three types of testimony you will take from witnesses who are called to testify at your evidentiary hearing: Direct, Cross-Examination and Redirect. Direct testimony is when you call the witness to the witness stand (as opposed to the State calling the witness) and are the first person to ask the witness questions. Cross-Examination testimony is when you are the person to ask the witness questions second. And redirect testimony comes after cross-examination testimony and is asked by the person who initially called the witness to testify.

With direct testimony you are asking the witness to paint a picture for the judge about whatever issue you are raising. You cannot "lead" a witness with your questions, which means you cannot suggest an answer in your question. For example, you cannot ask on direct examination: "Isn't it true that I told my lawyer that I wanted to accept the plea agreement?" That is a leading question that will be objected to by the prosecutor. You would have to ask something like, "Do you know what I told my lawyer about accepting a plea agreement?" In other words, you cannot ask "yes or no" questions with direct testimony.

Direct testimony can be harder to take than cross-examination testimony because with cross-examination testimony you can (and should) ask "yes or no" questions. With cross-examination testimony, you want to lead the witness right to the answer you want with your questions without the witness giving a narrative (long story) for their answer. And you never (or hardly ever) want to ask the question, "why?" This question opens the door for the witness to say whatever they want and explain their actions or inactions however they way. Most cross-examination questions begin with, "Isn't it true..."

CRITICAL TIP: Witnesses who you are cross-examining are against your position and do not want to help you out at all. You have to be careful of the questions you are asking them and only ask questions you know the answers to.

The party who initially called the witness to the stand takes redirect testimony. Redirect testimony is optional and is only used to clarify answers given on cross-examination. Redirect testimony must be limited to the answers/issues raised on cross-examination.

G. THE DECISION BY THE FEDERAL COURT

If you have an evidentiary hearing, then the court will take the matter under advisement, which means that a written decision will come out at a later date. At the start of your case, prior to the evidentiary hearing, you will be asked if you want to consent to a magistrate judge presiding over your case or if you want a district court judge to do so.

1. Magistrate Judge vs. District Court Judge

Magistrate judges are authorized to perform the full range of duties provided for magistrate judges under Title 28 U.S.C § 636. The court encourages civil litigants to consent to the jurisdiction of magistrate judges for all purposes up to final judgment, with any appeal directly to the Ninth Circuit Court of Appeals.

Magistrate judges are real judges authorized by statute. The only major difference is the manner in which magistrate judges are selected and the length of appointment. One is a political process— nomination by the President of the United States and confirmation by the Senate Judiciary Committee for a lifetime appointment— and the other is a merit selection process in which the magistrate judge is vetted fully by a committee selected by the district judges before the finalists are interviewed by the entire district court bench.

It is more beneficial to consent to a magistrate judge to consider your case and issue a Report and Recommendation to the district court judge. Since the magistrate judge's caseload is not as large as that of a district judge, they can spend more time on each case and have more flexibility. If you are going to get a hearing, you can generally obtain earlier hearings dates, and they have more time to allot to hearings. Also, you can have two bites at the apple: 1) the magistrate judge will consider your case and possibly rule in your favor; and 2) if the magistrate judge does not rule in your favor and recommends to the district court judge to deny your petition, the district court judge will review your case and the recommendation and make their own ruling.

2. Report and Recommendations

If you have chosen to let a magistrate judge consider your case, then you will receive a Report and Recommendation. This is referred to as, "R & R's." The magistrate's Report and Recommendation tells the district court judge how they should ultimately decide your case.

The Report and Recommendation will be a detailed ruling from the magistrate judge that addresses each of your arguments and explains why they should or should not be granted.

If the magistrate judge issues a Report and Recommendation that indicates that your petition should be denied, then it is imperative that you file an objection to the Report and Recommendation.

3. Objections to the Report and Recommendations

If you disagree with the Report and Recommendation, then you will have 14 days to file an objection. It is very important that your objection to the Report and Recommendation be detailed and specific as to what aspects of the magistrate's findings and rulings you are objecting to. If you are not specific, the district judge will simply affirm the magistrate's findings and recommendations.

For example, if you make general objections or simply repeat your arguments that were presented in the habeas petition, then the district court will issue an order with language such as, "The Magistrate Judge's Report recommends that the petition for writ of habeas corpus should be denied. Mr. Jarmon has filed objections to Magistrate Judge Hart's Report, but the objections consist merely of reiterating arguments previously made, asserting general disagreement with various aspects of the Report, or asserting boilerplate "legal" objections that provide no actual support for his claims, or are not responsive to Magistrate Judge Hart's conclusions. The Court concludes that the record review and analysis Magistrate Judge Hart conducted was entirely appropriate, that he correctly resolved all issues in this action, and that none of Mr. Jarmon's objections have any conceivable merit. Accordingly, Mr. Jarmon's petition will be denied."

As you can see from the ruling above, the petitioner failed to adequately object and the district court highlighted how the petitioner simply reiterated his arguments, made general disagreements, and asserted boilerplate objections. Your objection will look very similar to a legal brief discussing the law cited by the magistrate, your specific facts, and how the magistrate made specific errors in their legal reasoning.

CRITICAL TIP: If you receive an unfavorable Report and Recommendation and are going to file objections, then you should file an application for a 30-day extension to file the objections. By doing so, you will have additional time to flush out strong legal arguments as to why the magistrate erred in their report.

Your objection to the Report and Recommendations should be crafted very carefully because if you are not successful in District Court, the brief written for the objection is likely to be the brief you use to file an appeal in the U.S. Circuit Court of Appeals. Therefore, you will want to treat the objection brief as though you are arguing to the appellate court and be as thorough as possible, addressing each fact and law the Report and Recommendation erred on. **(See, Form #3 – Objection to Report and Recommendation Sample)**

4. CERTIFICATE OF APPEALABILITY

If the district court judge dismisses your petition, then you don't automatically get a chance to file an appeal to the U.S. Circuit Court of Appeals. You have to get permission to file an appeal. You get that permission by obtaining what is called a Certificate of Appealability, or "COA."

In order to obtain a COA you must file an application (or argument) for a COA. **(See, Form #4 – Application for Certificate of Appealability).** If the District Court denies the COA application, you can then file a motion for a

COA in the U.S. Circuit Court of Appeals. (The deadline to apply for a COA in the Ninth Circuit is 35 days after the date of the District Court's order denying a COA in that court). If neither court grants a COA, then the only remaining option is to try to obtain one from the U.S. Supreme Court – something that is theoretically possible, but which hardly ever occurs in practice.

The application for a Certificate of Appealability is a mini-brief of your case but focused only on how the magistrate or district judge decided your case. The standard to meet in order to obtain a COA is not too high. Under *Miller-El v. Cockrell*, 537 U.S. 322 (2003), you need not show that you are probably correct, or even that there is a substantial likelihood that you are correct in order to obtain a Certificate of Appealability.

The standard for a COA is if you can demonstrate that reasonable jurists would find the district court's assessment of your claim debatable. *Miller-El v. Cockrell*, 537 U.S. 322, 338 (2003). You can also have a certificate of appealability issue if the issues you present are "'adequate to deserve encouragement to proceed further.'" *Slack v. McDaniel*, 529 U.S. 473, 484 (2000)(quoting *Barefoot v. Estelle*, 463 U.S. 880, 893, n.4 (1983)).

The Ninth Circuit explained in *Jennings v. Woodford*, 290 F.3d 1006 (9th Cir. 2002), that the standard required for a COA is "relatively low." Id., at 1011, citing *Slack*. The following factors will determine if a COA issues in your case: (1) the issues are debatable among reasonable jurists; (2) another court could resolve the issues differently; or (3) the questions raised are adequate enough to encourage the petitioner to proceed further. Also, keep in mind (an argue in your brief) that "The court must resolve doubts about the propriety of a COA in the peti-tioner's favor." *Jennings, supra*, citing *Lambright v. Stewart*, 220 F.3d 1022, 1025 (9th Cir. 2000).

In your application for a COA, you will need to be precise with the facts and law of your case and explain why your case deserves to continue to the U.S. Court of Appeals using the standard and factors noted above.

H. Going to Circuit Court of Appeals

If you are successful in obtaining a Certificate of Appealability, the next step is to file an appeal from the District Court's final ruling. While another Manual could be written for preparing an appellate brief for the U.S. Circuit Courts of Appeal, this Manual will provide the steps needed to file the appellate brief.

Your appeal will be filed with one of the United States Circuit Courts of Appeal. There are eleven circuit courts in the United States. You have to file your appeal in the correct circuit. Below is a list of the circuit courts of appeal and the districts they serve. Remember, the "districts" are either states or part of states; some states are divided into separate districts.

First Circuit
Office of the Clerk
U.S. Court of Appeals
1 Courthouse Way, Suite 2500
Boston, MA 02210

The United States Court of Appeals for the 1st Circuit contains the following districts: District of Maine, District of Massachusetts, District of New Hampshire, District of Puerto Rico and District of Rhode Island.

Second Circuit
Thurgood Marshall U.S. Courthouse
40 Foley Square
New York, NY 10007

The United States Court of Appeals for the 2nd Circuit contains the following districts: District of Connecticut, Eastern District of New York, Northern District of New York, Southern District of New York, Western District of New York and the District of Vermont.

Third Circuit
U.S. Court of Appeals
Third Circuit
21400 U.S. Courthouse
601 Market Street
Philadelphia, PA 19106

The United States Court of Appeals for the 3rd Circuit contains the following districts: District of Delaware, District of New Jersey, Eastern District of Pennsylvania, Middle District of Pennsylvania and the Western District of Pennsylvania.

Fourth Circuit
Patricia S. Connor, Clerk
U.S. Court of Appeals for the Fourth Circuit
1100 East Main Street, Suite 501
Richmond, Virginia 23219

The United States Court of Appeals for the 4th Circuit contains the following districts: District of Maryland, Eastern District of North Carolina, Middle District of North Carolina, Western District of North Carolina, District of South Carolina, Eastern District of Virginia, Western District of Virginia, Northern District of West Virginia and the Southern District of West Virginia.

Fifth Circuit
U.S. Court of Appeals
For The Fifth Circuit
600 S. Maestri Place
Suite 115
New Orleans, LA 70130

The United States Court of Appeals for the 5th Circuit contains the following districts: Eastern District of Louisiana, Middle District of Louisiana, Western District of Louisiana, Northern District of Mississippi, Southern District of Mississippi, Eastern District of Texas, Northern District of Texas, Southern District of Texas and the Western District of Texas.

Sixth Circuit
Office of the Clerk
United States Court of Appeals for the Sixth Circuit
540 Potter Stewart U.S.Courthouse
100 E. Fifth Street
Cincinnati, Ohio 45202

The United States Court of Appeals for the 6th Circuit contains the following districts: Eastern District of Kentucky, Western District of Kentucky, Eastern District of Michigan, Western District of Michigan, Northern District of Ohio, Southern District of Ohio, Eastern District of Tennessee, Middle District of Tennessee and the Western District of Tennessee.

Seventh Circuit
United States Court of Appeals
for the Seventh Circuit
Everett McKinley Dirksen
United States Courthouse
219 S. Dearborn Street
Room 2722
Chicago, IL 60604

The United States Court of Appeals for the 7th Circuit contains the following districts: Central District of Illinois, Northern District of Illinois, Southern District of Illinois, Northern District of Indiana, Southern District of Indiana, Eastern District of Wisconsin and the Western District of Wisconsin.

Eighth Circuit
Thomas F. Eagleton Courthouse
111 South 10th Street
Room 24.329
St. Louis, MO. 63102

The United States Court of Appeals for the 8th Circuit contains the following districts: Eastern District of Arkansas, Western District of Arkansas, Northern District of Iowa, Southern District of Iowa, District of Minnesota, Eastern District of Missouri, Western District of Missouri, District of Nebraska, District of North Dakota and the District of South Dakota.

Ninth Circuit
The James R. Browning Courthouse
95 7th Street,
San Francisco, CA 94103

The United States Court of Appeals for the Ninth Circuit contains the following districts: District of Alaska, District of Arizona, Central District of California, Eastern District of California, Northern District of California, Southern District of California, District of Hawaii, District of Idaho, District of Montana, District of Nevada, District of Oregon, Eastern District of Washington and the Western District of Washington.

Tenth Circuit
Byron White U.S. Courthouse
1823 Stout Street
Denver, CO 80257

The United States Court of Appeals for the 10th Circuit contains the following districts: District of Colorado, District of Kansas, District of New Mexico, Eastern District of Oklahoma, Northern District of Oklahoma, Western District of Oklahoma, District of Utah and the District of Wyoming.

Eleventh Circuit
Elbert P. Tuttle Courthouse
56 Forsyth Street, N.W.
Atlanta, GA 30303

The United States Court of Appeals for the 11th Circuit contains the following districts: Middle District of Alabama, Northern District of Alabama, Southern District of Alabama, Middle District of Florida, Northern District of Florida, Southern District of Florida, Middle District of Georgia, Northern District of Georgia and the Southern District of Georgia.

Appeal to the Circuit Court

The appeal you file to the circuit court of appeal in your district is going to be an appeal from the decision of the district court. The caption of your appeal will be something to the effect of, "On Appeal From the United States District Court for the District of Arizona." Of course, you would put the district you are appealing from if it is not the District of Arizona.

For the body of the appellate brief, you will include a Table of Contents, a Table of Authorities, a Jurisdictional Statement, a Statement of Issues, a Statement of the Case, a Statement of the Facts, a Summary of Arguments, and then the Argument section. **(See, Form #5 – Sample Appellate Brief to the Ninth Circuit Court of Appeals)**.

Those sections are likely to be almost identical to the brief you filed in District Court and a version of the brief you filed to obtain a Certificate of Appealability. The reason your brief can be somewhat cut-and-pasted from your other briefs is because the court of appeals in habeas corpus actions reviews your issues de novo. "De novo" review means the court of appeals will consider the issues for the first time and without any deference to the district court's ruling. *Jensen v. Pliler*, 439 F.3d 1086, 1088 (9th Cir. 2006).

CRITICAL TIP: When drafting your appeal, you should also focus on the District Court's reasoning and explain why the reasoning is faulty. This argument will likely be in your objections to the Report and Recommendation that you filed in District Court. By addressing the District Court's reasoning in your brief, you'll get ahead of the prosecution when they file their response to your appellate brief.

APPENDIX A

28 U.S.C. § 2254; State Custody, Remedies in Federal Court

(a) The Supreme Court, a Justice thereof, a circuit judge, or a district court shall entertain an application for a writ of habeas corpus in behalf of a person in custody pursuant to the judgment of a State court only on the ground that he is in custody in violation of the Constitution or laws or treaties of the United States.

(b)(1) An application for a writ of habeas corpus on behalf of a person in custody pursuant to the judgment of a State court shall not be granted unless it appears that—

> **(A) the applicant has exhausted the remedies available in the courts of the State; or**
>
> **(B)(i) there is an absence of available State corrective process; or**
>
> **(ii) circumstances exist that render such process ineffective to protect the rights of the applicant.**

(2) An application for a writ of habeas corpus may be denied on the merits, notwithstanding the failure of the applicant to exhaust the remedies available in the courts of the State.

(3) A State shall not be deemed to have waived the exhaustion requirement or be estopped from reliance upon the requirement unless the State, through counsel, expressly waives the requirement.

(c) An applicant shall not be deemed to have exhausted the remedies available in the courts of the State, within the meaning of this section, if he has the right under the law of the State to raise, by any available procedure, the question presented.

(d) An application for a writ of habeas corpus on behalf of a person in custody pursuant to the judgment of a State court shall not be granted with respect to any claim that was adjudicated on the merits in State court proceedings unless the adjudication of the claim—

(1) resulted in a decision that was contrary to, or involved an unreasonable application of, clearly established Federal law, as determined by the Supreme Court of the United States; or

(2) resulted in a decision that was based on an unreasonable determination of the facts in light of the evidence presented in the State court proceeding.

(e)(1) In a proceeding instituted by an application for a writ of habeas corpus by a person in custody pursuant to the judgment of a State court, a determination of a factual issue made by a State court shall be presumed to be correct. The applicant shall have the burden of rebutting the presumption of correctness by clear and convincing evidence.

(2) If the applicant has failed to develop the factual basis of a claim in State court proceedings, the court shall not hold an evidentiary hearing on the claim unless the applicant shows that—

(A) the claim relies on—

(i) a new rule of constitutional law, made retroactive to cases on collateral review by the Supreme Court, that was previously unavailable; or

(ii) a factual predicate that could not have been previously discovered through the exercise of due diligence; and

(B) the facts underlying the claim would be sufficient to establish by clear and convincing evidence that but for constitutional error, no reasonable factfinder would have found the applicant guilty of the underlying offense.

(f) If the applicant challenges the sufficiency of the evidence adduced in such State court proceeding to support the State court's determination of a factual issue made therein, the applicant, if able, shall produce that part of the record pertinent to a determination of the sufficiency of the evidence to support such determination. If the applicant, because of indigency or other reason is unable to produce such part of the record, then the State shall produce such part of the record and the Federal court shall direct the State to do so by order directed to an appropriate State official. If the State cannot provide such pertinent part of the record, then the court shall determine under the existing facts and circumstances what weight shall be given to the State court's factual determination.

(g) A copy of the official records of the State court, duly certified by the clerk of such court to be a true and correct copy of a finding, judicial opinion, or other reliable written indicia showing such a factual determination by the State court shall be admissible in the Federal court proceeding.

(h) Except as provided in section 408 of the Controlled Substances Act, in all proceedings brought under this section, and any subsequent proceedings on review, the court may appoint counsel for an applicant who is or becomes financially unable to afford counsel, except as provided by a rule promulgated by the Supreme Court pursuant to statutory authority. Appointment of counsel under this section shall be governed by section 3006A of title 18.

(i) The ineffectiveness or incompetence of counsel during Federal or State collateral post-conviction proceedings shall not be a ground for relief in a proceeding arising under section 2254.

CASE LAW SYNOPSES

The following case law synopses are provided as a part of this Manual. The synopses are a brief statement as to what the cases hold and their application to habeas corpus law. For a better understanding of the case and how it relates to your particular case, you should read the full case and any other cases relating to the case. **These case synopses are provided as guidance only and should not be solely relied upon to support your legal arguments.**

Constitutional Issues Relating to Habeas Corpus

Standards of review prescribed by Antiterrorism and Effective Death Penalty Act (AEDPA) are not unconstitutional, notwithstanding claim that such standards violate the command of Article III by delegating the final exercise of federal judicial power to decide federal constitutional issues to state court. Hughes v. Johnson, C.A.5 (Tex.) 1999, 191 F.3d 607, certiorari denied 120 S.Ct. 1003, 528 U.S. 1145, 145 L.Ed.2d 945.

Statute giving finding of state postconviction court presumption of correctness in federal habeas corpus proceeding was not unconstitutional suspension of the writ to extent it required district court to defer to state court's assessment of witness' recantation testimony; recantation testimony did not affirmatively exonerate defendant but merely called into question validity of witness' identification of defendant. Landano v. Rafferty, C.A.3 (N.J.) 1988, 856 F.2d 569, certiorari denied 109 S.Ct. 1127, 489 U.S. 1014, 103 L.Ed.2d 189.

Provision of Antiterrorism and Effective Death Penalty Act (AEDPA) restricting scope of habeas review of state court decisions by lower federal courts to clearly established federal law as determined by the Supreme Court did not violate Article III; Congress could properly limit the sources of information a federal court could take into account when making a decision. Bowling v. Parker, E.D.Ky.2012, 882 F.Supp.2d 891.

Amendment to federal habeas corpus statute requiring more deference to state court's decision involving mixed questions of law and fact did not violate constitutional requirement of independent judiciary. Rodriguez v. Zavaras, D.Colo.1999, 42 F.Supp.2d 1059.

State prisoner was required to rely on § 2254, not § 2241, in challenging legality of execution of his sentence, under rule that more specific statute governs over more general, where allowing him to proceed under latter, more general authority, would have thwarted Congressional intent to restrict availability of second and successive petitions by state habeas petitioners. Coady v. Vaughn, C.A.3 (Pa.) 2001, 251 F.3d 480

Petition for writ of habeas corpus, rather than action under § 1983, was appropriate remedy for parolee seeking release from one of restrictions imposed by his parole, i.e., a ban on international travel, so that he could travel to foreign country to marry woman with whom he had been corresponding while incarcerated. Williams v. Wisconsin, C.A.7 (Wis.) 2003, 336 F.3d 576 .

Proper remedy in case involving inadequate medical treatment to pretrial detainee is relief under § 1983, not writ of habeas corpus. Rodney v. Romano, E.D.N.Y.1993, 814 F.Supp. 311

Prison Litigation Reform Act

The Prison Litigation Reform Act (PLRA) does not apply to habeas actions. Sonnier v. Johnson, C.A.5 (Tex.) 1998, 161 F.3d 941

Federal Rules of Civil Procedure

State prisoner seeking federal habeas relief from his murder conviction, on ground that the prosecution's concealment of hair comparison tests was a Brady violation, was entitled to discovery of the search warrant issued prior to his trial for the extraction of his head hair. Steward v. Grace, E.D.Pa.2005, 362 F.Supp.2d 608

Section of Anti-Terrorism and Effective Death Penalty Act (AEDPA) restricting evidentiary hearings on habeas claims did not modify rule governing expansion of record; the two provisions were not at cross-purposes but served different, albeit related, purposes. McNair v. Haley, M.D.Ala.2000, 97 F.Supp.2d 1270

Purpose of AEDPA

One of the purposes of the Antiterrorism and Effective Death Penalty Act of 1996 (AEDPA) is to reduce delays in the execution of state and federal criminal sentences, particularly in capital cases. Rhines v. Weber, U.S.2005, 125 S.Ct. 1528, 544 U.S. 269, 161 L.Ed.2d 440 , on remand 409 F.3d 982 .
Purpose of amendments to habeas corpus statute effected by Antiterrorism and Effective Death Penalty Act (AEDPA) was to reduce delays in execution of state and federal criminal sentences, particularly in capital cases, and to further principles of comity, finality, and federalism. Woodford v. Garceau, U.S.2003, 123 S.Ct. 1398, 538 U.S. 202, 155 L.Ed.2d 363 , on remand 399 F.3d 1101

Retroactivity

Inmate's petition for habeas corpus relief was governed by Antiterrorism and Effective Death Penalty Act (AEDPA), where petition was filed after effective date of Act. Pursell v. Horn, W.D.Pa.2002, 187 F.Supp.2d 260

Antiterrorism and Effective Death Penalty Act (AEDPA) applied to habeas petition filed after its effective date despite facts that alleged constitutional violations for which petitioner sought relief occurred prior to its effective date and that petitioner filed his appeal prior to its effective date. Mitchell v. Ward, W.D.Okla.1999, 150 F.Supp.2d 1194 , as amended, certificate of appealability denied 1999 WL 33316065 , affirmed in part, reversed in part 262 F.3d 1036 , appeal after remand from federal court 136 P.3d 671 , appeal after new sentencing hearing 235 P.3d 640 , certiorari denied 131 S.Ct. 1688, 179 L.Ed.2d 627

United States Supreme Court's Crawford decision, which overruled prior Supreme Court case governing admission of hearsay statements in criminal trials over Confrontation Clause objection, did not announce “watershed rule” of criminal procedure, such as could be applied retroactively on collateral review, where overall effect of Crawford with regard to accuracy of fact-finding in criminal cases was not easy to assess, and it could not be said that application of rule announced in Crawford was necessary to prevent impermissibly large risk of inaccurate conviction, and where the Crawford rule lacked the primacy and centrality required to be regarded as having altered courts' understanding of bedrock procedural elements essential to fairness of proceeding. Whorton v. Bockting, U.S.2007, 127 S.Ct. 1173, 549 U.S. 406, 167 L.Ed.2d 1 .

To apply rule of Teague v. Lane, that new rule of constitutional law established after conviction has become final generally cannot be used to attack conviction, federal court: (1) must determine date upon which conviction became final; (2) must survey legal landscape as it then existed and determine whether state court considering defendant's claim at time conviction became final would have felt compelled by existing precedent to conclude that rule he or she seeks was required by Constitution; and (3) must, if it determines that habeas petitioner seeks benefit of new rule, consider whether relief sought falls within one of the two narrow exceptions to nonretroactivity. Lambrix v. Singletary, U.S.Fla.1997, 117 S.Ct. 1517, 520 U.S. 518, 137 L.Ed.2d 771

The Teague rule is a “nonretroactivity principle” that prevents a federal court from granting habeas corpus relief to a state prisoner based on a rule announced after his conviction and sentence became final. Smith v. Roe, C.D.Cal.2002, 232 F.Supp.2d 1073

Supreme Court's holding in Martinez v. Ryan, that, in some circumstances, the ineffective effective assistance of state post-conviction relief counsel can serve as cause to excuse the procedural default of an ineffective-assistance-of-trial-counsel claim, was not a constitutional decision, and, therefore, it could not underpin a second or successive habeas corpus petition based on a new rule of constitutional law; Martinez did not expressly overrule any prior decision, but rather qualified Coleman v. Thompson by recognizing a narrow exception to that case's rule that state post-conviction relief counsel's ineffective assistance could not serve as cause to excuse the procedural default of an ineffective-assistance-of-trial-counsel claim, and, moreover, the Supreme Court in Martinez characterized its decision as an "equitable ruling," and not a "constitutional" one. Jones v. Ryan, C.A.9 (Ariz.) 2013, 733 F.3d 825 , certiorari denied 134 S.Ct. 503, 571 U.S. 984, 187 L.Ed.2d 340 .

Function of Writ

Function of federal habeas corpus is to test by way of original civil proceeding, independent of normal channels of review of criminal judgments, the very gravest allegations, and state prisoners are entitled to relief only on proving that their detention violates the fundamental liberties of the person, safeguarded against state action by United States Constitution. Townsend v. Sain, U.S.Ill.1963, 83 S.Ct. 745, 372 U.S. 293, 9 L.Ed.2d 770 . See, also, Roy v. Hall, C.A.1 (Mass.) 1975, 521 F.2d 120 .
Awesome power of writ of habeas corpus to avoid res judicata, and its implications for federalism, demand that its use be confined to its proper role of preservation of individual liberty and relief from unlawful custody. (Per Garth, Circuit Judge, with three Judges concurring, two Judges concurring in separate opinions and four Judges dissenting.) Lehman v. Lycoming County Children's Services Agency, C.A.3 (Pa.) 1981, 648 F.2d 135 , certiorari granted 102 S.Ct. 89, 454 U.S. 813, 70 L.Ed.2d 82 , affirmed 102 S.Ct. 3231, 458 U.S. 502, 73 L.Ed.2d 928

Function of habeas corpus review is not to retry a case, but merely to review previous trial to insure that justice has been done. U.S. ex rel. Clemmer v. Mazurkiewicz, E.D.Pa.1973, 365 F.Supp. 1158 , affirmed 487 F.2d 1396 , certiorari denied 94 S.Ct. 1440, 415 U.S. 929, 39 L.Ed.2d 487

Convicted state prisoner could seek DNA testing of crime-scene evidence based on due process in § 1983 action; success in suit for DNA testing would not necessarily imply unlawfulness of State's custody, and thus habeas was not exclusive remedy; abrogating Harvey v. Horan, 278 F.3d 370, Kutzner v. Montgomery County, 303 F.3d 339. Skinner v. Switzer, U.S.2011, 131 S.Ct. 1289, 562 U.S. 521, 179 L.Ed.2d 233, on remand 425 Fed.Appx. 409, 2011 WL 1885622

Habeas corpus is not a rigid and inflexible proceeding in which court must either order release of prisoner outright or direct his return to custody. U.S. ex rel. D'Amico v. Bishopp, C.A.2 (N.Y.) 1961, 286 F.2d 320, certiorari denied 81 S.Ct. 1924, 366 U.S. 963, 6 L.Ed.2d 1254.

Civil Case, Not Criminal

A habeas petition submitted by a state prisoner initiates a civil, rather than criminal, action for relief; therefore, no case or controversy generally exists before an actual habeas petition is filed. U.S. v. Thomas, C.A.3 (Pa.) 2013, 713 F.3d 165, certiorari denied 133 S.Ct. 2873, 570 U.S. 927, 186 L.Ed.2d 926

Habeas corpus proceeding in federal court is civil action contesting legality of restraint of petitioner's personal liberty at which guilt or innocence is not to be redetermined, nor is the proceeding an additional avenue of appeal, and it is only when circumstances are presented which demonstrate fundamental unfairness in trial, or the infringement of important constitutional rights, that questions of federal dimension arise warranting intrusion into the province of a state's criminal courts. U.S. ex rel. Rush v. Ziegele, D.N.J.1971, 335 F.Supp. 434.

Habeas corpus is a civil remedy which tests legality of petitioner's detention and is justified when petitioner is in custody in violation of Constitution or laws of United States. Grant v. Swenson, E.D.Mo.1970, 313 F.Supp. 1117.

Collateral Attack

This section regarding applications for writs of habeas corpus by persons in custody pursuant to state court judgment applies only to collateral attacks on state court judgments. McGuire v. Blubaum, D.C.Ariz.1974, 376 F.Supp. 284.

Petition for habeas corpus in federal court by Maryland state prisoner is collateral proceeding only. Mason v. Warden, Md. Penitentiary, D.C.Md.1962, 208 F.Supp. 777.

Appointment of Counsel

There is neither a constitutional nor statutory right to counsel in federal habeas proceedings; instead, the appointment is committed to the discretion of the trial court. Creek v. Weber, D.S.D.2009, 598 F.Supp.2d 1004.

Duty of the Court

Pursuant to Antiterrorism and Effective Death Penalty Act (AEDPA), a state habeas petitioner can succeed if he demonstrates that the state court judgment was either contrary to or an unreasonable application of federal law; in the event there is no state court decision on the merits of the issue, federal appellate court is required to dispose of the matter as law and justice require. Guest v. McCann, C.A.7 (Ill.) 2007, 474 F.3d 926, rehearing and suggestion for rehearing en banc denied, certiorari denied 128 S.Ct. 170, 552 U.S. 824, 169 L.Ed.2d 33.

Duty of federal court on habeas corpus is to ensure that state criminal proceedings conform to federal constitutional standards. Turnbow v. Estelle, C.A.5 (Tex.) 1975, 510 F.2d 127.

Court of appeals has responsibility to assure that state prisoner seeking federal habeas corpus obtains fair trial by impartial jury. Bruce v. Estelle, C.A.5 (Tex.) 1973, 483 F.2d 1031.

It is always the duty of a federal court to grant habeas relief whenever it independently determines that a person is in custody in violation of the Constitution or laws or treaties of the United States. Stone v. Wainwright, C.A.5 (Fla.) 1973, 478 F.2d 390, reversed on other grounds 94 S.Ct. 190, 414 U.S. 21, 38 L.Ed.2d 179.

Time for Decision

This section provides for swift, flexible and summary determination of state prisoner's claim. Preiser v. Rodriguez, U.S.N.Y.1973, 93 S.Ct. 1827, 411 U.S. 475, 36 L.Ed.2d 439.

Even if 31-month delay to dispose of habeas petition was unreasonable, remedy for any such delay did not include overturning of petitioner's otherwise valid state court conviction. Moya v. Estelle, C.A.5 (Tex.) 1983, 696 F.2d 329.

Writ of habeas corpus must be construed to afford swift and imperative remedy in all cases of illegal restraint or confinement; writ is reduced to sham if trial courts do not act within reasonable time. Jones v. Shell, C.A.8 (Ark.) 1978, 572 F.2d 1278.

Federal habeas corpus court was without authority to defer action on petitioner's habeas corpus case and other habeas corpus actions pending before him to await ruling by the United States Supreme Court in another case. McClellan v. Young, C.A.6 (Ohio) 1970, 421 F.2d 690.

Petition for Habeas Corpus

Petitions to set aside guilty pleas must strictly comply with requirements that there be some evidentiary "spelling out" of the basic claim of a coerced plea and that the precise claim presented to federal court must also have been presented to and ruled upon by the state court. U.S. ex rel. Gentile v. Mancusi, C.A.2 (N.Y.) 1970, 426 F.2d 238, certiorari denied 91 S.Ct. 248, 400 U.S. 944, 27 L.Ed 2d 249.

There should not be a rigid formalism in habeas corpus proceedings in which courts are seeking substance as to violation of constitutional rights, but it must be remembered that habeas corpus is a collateral attack by courts of federal jurisdiction invading province of state jurisdiction, and trial of competency of counsel is only a phase of his collateral attack, and to warrant such collateral investigations of competency of counsel, the pleadings should lay a foundation therefor by proper factual averments, and competent evidence must clearly support such averments. Davis v. Bomar, C.A.6 (Tenn.) 1965, 344 F.2d 84, certiorari denied 86 S.Ct. 177, 382 U.S. 883, 15 L.Ed.2d 124.

Habeas petitioner was required to fairly identify, in his petition, any prevailing federal law from the United States Supreme Court which was allegedly ignored or misapplied by the state courts' rejection of his claim that prosecution's use of jailhouse informants violated his due process rights. Hannon v. Secretary, Department of Corrections, M.D.Fla.2007, 622 F.Supp.2d 1169, certificate of appealability denied 2008 WL 58958, affirmed 562 F.3d 1146, certiorari denied 130 S.Ct. 504, 558 U.S. 997, 175 L.Ed.2d 358.

Petitioners in habeas corpus must come forward with some factual allegations to support legal contentions. Lunnermon v. Peyton, W.D.Va.1970, 310 F.Supp. 323, affirmed 440 F.2d 774.

State prisoner's motion to amend his federal petition for writ of habeas corpus to assert a claim that the Minnesota Department of Corrections violated his due process rights by deleting parts of a security tape, thus spoliating evidence, and a claim that impermissible evidence was admitted at his criminal trial in violation of his Miranda rights, would be denied as futile, where prisoner failed to exhaust either claim in state court by appealing them to the Minnesota Supreme Court or raising them in a postconviction relief proceeding, and both claims were claims that prisoner should have known about and raised at the time of his direct appeal. Latimer v. Smith, D.Minn.2018, 351 F.Supp.3d 1218.

Petitioner engaged in undue delay in seeking amendment to habeas petition to add claims of ineffective assistance of counsel, where petitioner did not amend after he filed motion to stay his federal habeas application to exhaust state remedies and two Antiterrorism and Effective Death Penalty Act (AEDPA) election forms issued by court provided petitioner with two separate opportunities to either amend his application or withdraw it without prejudice so that he could file one all-inclusive habeas application after exhausting state remedies but he did not ask to amend application then either. Hall v. Phelps, D.Del.2009, 641 F.Supp.2d 334.

Petitioner was not entitled to amend his habeas petition to add claims which were denied by state postconviction court on basis of exclusive reliance on "adequate and independent" state procedural rule; because petitioner was not able to demonstrate any attempt to establish cause and prejudice, or factual innocence, permitting amendment of the petition to include those claims would be futile. Mills v. Girdich, W.D.N.Y.2009, 614 F.Supp.2d 365.

Pro Se Petition for Habeas Corpus

A pro se federal habeas petitioner's submissions should be held to less stringent standards than formal pleadings drafted by lawyers. Bell v. Ercole, S.D.N.Y.2009, 631 F.Supp.2d 406.

Even if pro se petition for writ of habeas corpus could be construed as a complaint, it failed to provide the required short and plain statement of the grounds upon which the court's jurisdiction depended or the required short and plain statement of the claim for relief. Grigsby v. Thomas, D.D.C.2007, 506 F.Supp.2d 26.

District court could disregard habeas petitioner's failure to sign habeas petition or include last page of form, rather than dismissing or returning petition, where defects appeared to be oversight, petitioner was appearing pro se, considerable time had passed since petition was filed, and claims tracked those that petitioner had made under oath in state court postconviction proceeding. Quinn v. Dooley, D.S.D.2003, 272 F.Supp.2d 839.

While courts should liberally interpret pro se habeas corpus pleadings with leniency and understanding, this should not place on reviewing court entire onus of creating federal claim for state prisoner. Burkey v. Deeds, D.Nev.1993, 824 F.Supp. 190

Sufficiency of Petition for Habeas Corpus

Petitioner presented in his petition for writ of habeas corpus ineffective assistance of counsel claim regarding petitioner's guilty plea in state court proceedings, requiring district court to address claim; petition asserted that attorney failed to go into detail about what it was petitioner failed to understand in plea agreement and allowed petitioner to testify on his own behalf under duress. Dupree v. Warden, C.A.11 (Ala.) 2013, 715 F.3d 1295, on remand 2015 WL 4274456.

Habeas petitioner's perfunctory reference, without discussion, that application by Missouri courts of Missouri's fugitive dismissal rule to facts of his case was incongruent with substantive due process did not bring issue before federal habeas court, and thus, habeas court declined to exercise its discretion to consider question of law on appeal. Schleeper v. Groose, C.A.8 (Mo.) 1994, 36 F.3d 735.

Petitioner failed to plead any claims warranting habeas corpus review, in view of vague and conclusory allegations in pro se habeas petition and response to state's answer to his petition; petitioner claimed that he was "falsely imprisoned" pursuant to "constitutionally vague" state statute, but failed to identify statute or explain facts behind alleged false imprisonment, petitioner attached state court motion for post-conviction relief that failed to assist court in that it alleged unrelated ineffective assistance of counsel claim and claim that police officer committed perjury, and petitioner's response to state's answer asserted new and unrelated allegation that he was denied medical care in prison, which was a challenge to condition of confinement not cognizable on habeas review. Simms v. Carroll, D.Del.2006, 432 F.Supp.2d 443.

District court would not address petitioner's claim as it related to jury selection videotape, in habeas petition under Antiterrorism and Effective Death Penalty Act (AEDPA), since court could not deduce whether petitioner's claim was exhausted or was procedurally defaulted based upon independent and adequate state procedural law grounds because petitioner neither informed court about reasons for state court's denial of his motion nor alleged that state court erred in denying application and motion. Porter v. Horn, E.D.Pa.2003, 276 F.Supp.2d 278.

State prisoner seeking to overturn conviction on ground that guilty plea was involuntary must present more persuasive and compelling testimony than his own unsupported interpretation of his state of mind. U.S. ex rel. Ward v. Deegan, S.D.N.Y.1970, 310 F.Supp. 1076.

Successive Petition for Habeas Corpus

A habeas petition which is filed after an initial petition was dismissed without adjudication on the merits for failure to exhaust state remedies is not a "second or successive petition" as that term is understood in the habeas corpus context, but federal courts retain broad powers to prevent duplicative or unnecessary litigation; abrogating Farmer v. McDaniel, 98 F.3d 1548. Slack v. McDaniel, U.S.Nev.2000, 120 S.Ct. 1595, 529 U.S. 473, 146 L.Ed.2d 542.

Nevada rule of procedure barring second or successive state habeas petitions asserting claims that were not raised previously was not regularly and consistently applied, and thus was inadequate to bar federal habeas review of petitioner's claim that trial court violated his due process rights at his capital murder trial by advising the jury that if it found premeditation, it had necessarily found deliberation. Riley v. McDaniel, C.A.9 (Nev.) 2015, 786 F.3d 719, certiorari denied 136 S.Ct. 1450, 577 U.S. 1229, 194 L.Ed.2d 575.

State capital defendant's motion for relief from judgment, based on claim regarding denial of motion for evidentiary development, was in substance an unauthorized second or successive habeas petition over which district court lacked jurisdiction, where substance of the claim was decided on the merits in prior habeas proceedings. Wood v. Ryan, C.A.9 (Ariz.) 2014, 759 F.3d 1117, certiorari denied 135 S.Ct. 21, 573 U.S. 977, 189 L.Ed.2d 873.

Colorado post-conviction court's application of Colorado's successive bar rule to deny petitioner's post-conviction Brady claim as, sub silentio, part and parcel of his newly discovered evidence claim, which was addressed and decided on direct appeal, did not affect the availability of federal habeas review of the Brady claim; petitioner raised a state-law non-disclosure claim on direct appeal and, based on the same facts, a Brady claim on post-conviction review, and the post-conviction court applied the state bar on successive claims in declining to reach the merits of the Brady claim. LeBere v. Abbott, C.A.10 (Colo.) 2013, 732 F.3d 1224.

A motion for relief from judgment, following the denial of a habeas petition, seeking leave to present newly discovered evidence in support of claim previously denied must be treated as successive petition for habeas corpus requiring an appellate court's authorization before filing. Sanders v. Norris, C.A.8 (Ark.) 2008, 529 F.3d 787, rehearing and rehearing en banc denied.

Petition for federal habeas corpus relief did not qualify as "second or successive petition" when previously filed petition was not adjudicated on the merits. Green v. White, C.A.9 (Cal.) 2000, 223 F.3d 1001.

Successive petition and abuse of writ doctrines did not bar habeas corpus petitioner from raising claim, even though claim had been raised in prior action, where claim had been dismissed pursuant to motion in which petitioner joined and court did not order dismissal based on deficiency of its merits. Rehbein v. Dahm, D.Neb.1994, 855 F.Supp. 1066, affirmed 94 F.3d 478, rehearing denied.

Inasmuch as defendant's motion to strike his original petition for post-conviction relief and first two amendments was never addressed by the state courts, his third amended petition should not have been treated as a successive petition prohibited by Ohio law, rather than as a permissible amendment of his original petition; thus, Brady claim raised in third amended petition was not procedurally defaulted for purposes of federal habeas review. Jalowiec v. Bradshaw, C.A.6 (Ohio) 2011, 657 F.3d 293, as amended, rehearing and rehearing en banc denied, certiorari denied 133 S.Ct. 107, 568 U.S. 828, 184 L.Ed.2d 49.

Amendment of habeas petition containing one exhausted claim to assert newly exhausted claims that had not been exhausted at time of filing of petition did not constitute second or "successive writ" under abuse of writ doctrine. Anthony v. Cambra, C.A.9 (Cal.) 2000, 236 F.3d 568, certiorari denied 121 S.Ct. 2576, 533 U.S. 941, 150 L.Ed.2d 739.

Motion to amend habeas petition to add additional claims that had been exhausted while petition was pending was not a second or successive petition. Brown v. Donelly, E.D.N.Y.2003, 258 F.Supp.2d 178.

Stay of Proceedings

The Antiterrorism and Effective Death Penalty Act (AEDPA) does not deprive the district court of its authority to issue a stay. Ryan v. Gonzales, U.S.2013, 133 S.Ct. 696, 568 U.S. 57, 184 L.Ed.2d 528, on remand 518 Fed.Appx. 441, 2013 WL 1663308.

Even assuming that habeas petitioner forfeited argument on appeal that magistrate judge lacked authority to issue final order on his motion to stay and abey his habeas petition while he exhausted new claim in state court because such ruling was dispositive as to his unexhausted claim, Court of Appeals would exercise its discretion to consider argument on appeal; issue of whether stay-and-abey motion was dispositive matter was purely legal one, record was fully developed on the issue, and petitioner never received any notice that magistrate judge had determined that the motion was not dispositive. Bastidas v. Chappell, C.A.9 (Cal.) 2015, 791 F.3d 1155.

Denial of petitioner's motion to stay and abey his habeas petition while he exhausted new claim not asserted in petition in state court was dispositive as to that new unexhausted claim, and thus magistrate judge lacked authority to issue final order denying motion, absent petitioner's consent, but rather was required to submit report and recommendation to district court; denial of the motion meant that petitioner would never be able to assert the new claim in federal habeas proceedings. Bastidas v. Chappell, C.A.9 (Cal.) 2015, 791 F.3d 1155.

Naming Proper Respondent

The state is not a proper respondent in a habeas corpus proceeding, given that state has sovereign immunity from suit in federal court, that rule governing habeas corpus petitions requires that respondent be the "state officer" having custody of the petitioner, and that designation of state could create confusion with respect to service and to notice generally. Bridges v. Chambers, C.A.7 (Ill.) 2005, 425 F.3d 1048.

Habeas petition challenging petitioner's confinement by the Department of Homeland Security (DHS) while deportation proceedings were pending was required to name respondents who directly controlled DHS facilities where he was confined or had immediate physical control over him. Excellent v. Ashcroft, S.D.N.Y.2005, 359 F.Supp.2d 333.

Right to Counsel

Petitioner for habeas corpus was not entitled to appointment of counsel, where all issues presented in petition were either successive or abusive, there was no conflicting testimony presented as to abusive claims, petitioner presented no evidence indicating that factual allegations warranted further investigation or that he did not have the ability to investigate facts further, the issues presented in petition were not either factually or legally complex, petition presented issues adequately and did not appear to be less coherent than most pro se petitions and district court was well able to extract claims presented, and there was no evidence that either petitioner or court would benefit from appointment of counsel. Nachtigall v. Class, C.A.8 (S.D.) 1995, 48 F.3d 1076.

Sixth Amendment guarantee of right to effective assistance of counsel applies only to criminal cases and not to petitions for habeas relief, which are civil in nature. Barkauskas v. Lane, C.A.7 (Ill.) 1991, 946 F.2d 1292.

While district court had discretion to appoint counsel to aid petitioner in his habeas corpus proceeding, failure to appoint counsel was not an abuse of discretion and did not violate any right of petitioner under U.S.C.A. Const. Amend. 6. Williams v. State of Mo., C.A.8 (Mo.) 1981, 640 F.2d 140, certiorari denied 101 S.Ct. 2328, 451 U.S. 990, 68 L.Ed.2d 849.

Since, even if both pharmacy robbery convictions were set aside, prisoner would still have two other valid convictions which would justify invocation of Missouri second offender statute upon a subsequent conviction, prisoner was not entitled to any habeas corpus relief even if his contentions with respect to the convictions were accepted so that his petition was frivolous and he was not entitled to appointment of counsel in connection with his petition for habeas corpus. Tyler v. Wyrick, C.A.8 (Mo.) 1976, 540 F.2d 921.

In proceeding for habeas corpus relief to compel state court to grant credit on sentence for time served in jail while awaiting trial, there was no error on part of United States district court in not appointing counsel. Martin v. State of Fla., C.A.5 (Fla.) 1976, 533 F.2d 270.

Though counsel serves on appeal in civil habeas corpus proceeding by discretionary appointment of court of appeals rather than because of declared constitutional right, it is appropriate to apply principles enunciated by Supreme Court in Anders v. California to determine whether appointed counsel should be allowed to withdraw. Dinkins v. State of Ala., C.A.5 (Ala.) 1976, 526 F.2d 1268, certiorari denied 97 S.Ct. 119, 429 U.S. 842, 50 L.Ed.2d 112.

Habeas corpus is civil action, and there is no constitutional right to assistance of counsel in such proceedings in federal court. Hopkins v. Anderson, C.A.10 (Okla.) 1974, 507 F.2d 530, certiorari denied 95 S.Ct. 1586, 421 U.S. 920, 43 L.Ed.2d 788.

Counsel is appointed on appeal and remains unless he can convince court that an appeal would be frivolous but on a habeas corpus petition accused must allege facts that convince court there is sufficient merit to his claim to warrant appointment of counsel. Jackson v. Turner, C.A.10 (Utah) 1971, 442 F.2d 1303.

Indigent state prisoner applying to federal court for habeas corpus is not entitled to appointed attorney unless particular circumstances indicate that it is necessary to obtain due process. Kreiling v. Field, C.A.9 (Cal.) 1970, 431 F.2d 638.

Where record of proceedings in state trial court, included as part of return to order to show cause in federal habeas corpus proceeding, showed that matter had been reliably determined by state court after full hearing and application did not disclose other unusual circumstances, petitioner was not entitled to court-appointed counsel on basis that he advanced constitutional questions of complexity and seriousness. Washa v. Eyman, C.A.9 (Ariz.) 1970, 429 F.2d 568.

State prisoner was not entitled to counsel in preparing and arguing his petition for writ of habeas corpus. Pope v. Turner, C.A.10 (Utah) 1970, 426 F.2d 783.

Denial of indigent state prisoner's motion for appointment of counsel to assist him in federal habeas corpus proceeding in district court was not error, in view of questions raised by petitioner and fact that he deliberately bypassed state remedies after being fully advised. Eskridge v. Rhay, C.A.9 (Wash.) 1965, 345 F.2d 778, certiorari denied 86 S.Ct. 582, 382 U.S. 996, 15 L.Ed.2d 483, rehearing denied 86 S.Ct. 903, 383 U.S. 922, 15 L.Ed.2d 679.

There is no constitutional right to representation by counsel in a habeas corpus proceeding in federal court. U.S. ex rel. Wissenfeld v. Wilkins, C.A.2 (N.Y.) 1960, 281 F.2d 707. See, also, Flowers v. State of Okl., C.A. 10 (Okl.) 1966, 356 F.2d 916; Rodriguez v. Nelson, D.C.Cal.1968, 286 F.Supp. 321.

There is no constitutional right to counsel in habeas actions. Quinn v. Dooley, D.S.D.2003, 272 F.Supp.2d 839.

Among standards to be considered in determining whether habeas petitioner should have appointed counsel are legal and factual merits of claim presented, degree of complexity of issues involved, and petitioner's apparent physical and intellectual abilities to prosecute action. Ballard v. Duckworth, N.D.Ind.1986, 656 F.Supp. 693, affirmed 815 F.2d 709

Hearing was not required to consider petitioner's habeas petition as grounds raised by petition were covered by trial record and were subject of evidentiary hearing in state court; thus, petitioner was not entitled to assistance of additional counsel for habeas petition. Beasley v. Holland, S.D.W.Va.1986, 649 F.Supp. 561, appeal dismissed 841 F.2d 1122, certiorari denied 109 S.Ct. 156, 488 U.S. 860, 102 L.Ed.2d 127.

Where issues were adequately presented by habeas corpus petitioner, petitioner was not entitled to appointment of counsel or of a legal assistant. Neeley v. Duckworth, N.D.Ind.1979, 473 F.Supp. 288.

An order of release or retrial should be followed by appointment of counsel at a meaningful time early enough so that defense can be prepared and retrial begun within time limits set by court; failure to make timely appointment whipsaws defendant between right to timely trial free of constitutional error resulting in original grant of habeas corpus relief and right to have counsel prepare and present adequate defense. Gardner v. Forister, W.D.N.C.1979, 472 F.Supp. 1.

Habeas corpus petitioner's tardy motion for appointment of counsel would be denied where action had been fully processed and was one which did not involve complex legal issues which petitioner could not comprehend. Miller v. State of Mo., W.D.Mo.1975, 394 F.Supp. 94.

State prisoner would not be permitted to represent himself in habeas corpus case and further proceedings would be ordered stayed indefinitely pending clarification as to status of his counsel, his sixth, with whom he had had a difference of opinion. Pruitt v. Peyton, E.D.Va.1965, 249 F.Supp. 276.

Continuance of Habeas Proceedings

Denial of continuance in habeas corpus proceeding, involving question of waiver of right to counsel, was abuse of discretion where petitioner had been committed to mental institution and was not available to testify. Alvis v. Kimbrough, C.A.5 (Fla.) 1972, 455 F.2d 922.

Right to Discovery During Habeas Proceedings

Denial of habeas petitioner's motion for leave to conduct discovery was not abuse of discretion when petitioner did not establish that requested discovery was unavailable during direct appeal and did not show that requested discovery would uncover evidence of constitutional violation. Beuke v. Houk, C.A.6 (Ohio) 2008, 537 F.3d 618, rehearing and rehearing en banc denied, certiorari denied 129 S.Ct. 2792, 557 U.S. 906, 174 L.Ed.2d 294.

New York state prisoner's application for discovery in his federal habeas corpus proceeding was broad and speculative, and thus he failed to demonstrate good cause to warrant requested discovery, where application merely listed his seven discovery requests without any discussion of their potential utility, and further, information he sought should have been produced or elicited during state criminal proceedings, and he neither claimed nor demonstrated any basis for concluding that he did not receive such information. Edwards v. Superintendent, Southport C.F., E.D.N.Y.2013, 991 F.Supp.2d 348, appeal dismissed.

Federal habeas petitioner failed to show good cause for discovery of transcribed copy of compact disc containing 911 call; disc did not contain information that would enable petitioner to demonstrate that he was entitled to relief, since it pertained only to his Fourth Amendment claim, which was fully and fairly presented in state court and could not form basis for relief. McClelland v. Kirkpatrick, W.D.N.Y.2011, 778 F.Supp.2d 316.

Detainee at Guantanamo Bay Naval Base was not entitled to production of documents, in habeas proceeding, concerning his physical or mental condition since he had been held in Guantanamo; detainee failed to demonstrate that such records would show that his detention was unlawful, and to extent that records detailed alleged abusive treatment, torture, or mental or physical incapacity, records would be produced pursuant to order requiring government to produce any and all available evidence of abusive treatment, torture, or mental or physical incapacity prior to or contemporaneous with time that detainee gave any statements that were contained in factual return. Lnu v. Obama, D.D.C.2009, 656 F.Supp.2d 187.

Detainee at Guantanamo Bay Naval Base was not entitled to production, in habeas proceeding, of documents related to his extraordinary rendition "prior to" his detention; detainee failed to show that requested documents would likely show that his detention was unlawful, and to extent government relied upon any statements made during rendition to justify detention, information regarding such statements was covered by prior district court order requiring government to produce all reasonably available records and reports of interrogations in which detainee made or adopted statements upon which government relied to justify detention. Lnu v. Obama, D.D.C.2009, 656 F.Supp.2d 187.

Guantanamo Bay Naval Base detainee's discovery requests, in habeas proceeding, seeking records and reports pertaining to his interrogation upon which government relied to support his detention satisfied "good cause" requirement of amended case management order (CMO) providing for rules of discovery, and thus detainee was entitled to requested discovery; requests were narrowly tailored to include only evidence upon which government relied, and detainee's access to evidence sought would likely demonstrate that his detention was unlawful. Lnu v. Obama, D.D.C.2009, 656 F.Supp.2d 187.

District Court would only consider, in habeas proceeding, discovery requests of detainee at Guantanamo Bay Naval Base insofar as they sought reasonably available evidence, since detainee did not specify where any of the discovery he sought was located, and amended case management order (CMO) providing for rules of discovery required that requests must not unfairly disrupt or unduly burden government. Lnu v. Obama, D.D.C.2009, 656 F.Supp.2d 187.

Habeas petitioner failed to demonstrate good cause as would permit discovery of information regarding denial of request for transfer to Israel, the country of petitioner's citizenship, pursuant to Transfer of Offenders to or from Foreign Countries Act, where transfer decision-making process was wholly discretionary such that further insight into considerations underlying denial of transfer would not affect petitioner's eligibility for habeas relief. Yosef v. Killian, S.D.N.Y.2009, 646 F.Supp.2d 499.

Good cause may be found, as required to obtain discovery in a federal habeas proceeding, when the petitioner establishes a prima facie claim for relief. Batiste v. Quarterman, S.D.Tex.2008, 622 F.Supp.2d 423.

For purposes of habeas petitioner's claims alleging Brady violations, good cause existed for habeas court to authorize habeas petitioner to conduct discovery with respect to all documents in the possession of the police relating to contact with, or investigation of, two individuals allegedly involved in the crimes and any other suspect or party of interest regarding the attempted murder or murder, including all jail, medical and mental health records. Williams v. Schriro, D.Ariz.2006, 423 F.Supp.2d 994.

A habeas petitioner, unlike the civil litigant in federal court, is not entitled to discovery as a matter of ordinary course. Steward v. Grace, E.D.Pa.2005, 362 F.Supp.2d 608.

Issues to be Reviewed in Habeas Proceedings

District court must resolve all claims for relief raised in petition for writ of habeas corpus, regardless of whether habeas relief is granted or denied. Clisby v. Jones, C.A.11 (Ala.) 1992, 960 F.2d 925.

Habeas corpus petitioner in federal court cannot merely characterize some state act as unconstitutional and expect federal court to explore all possible grounds under each article and amendment of the Federal Constitution. Burkey v. Deeds, D.Nev.1993, 824 F.Supp. 190.

Petition for habeas corpus, not petitioner's brief, controls issues which may be raised and which court will address. Neal v. Grammer, D.Neb.1991, 769 F.Supp. 1523, affirmed 975 F.2d 463.

Upon habeas corpus, court may look only for violation of right secured to petitioner by United States Constitution and not for trial errors that might call for application of supervisory powers of an appellate court. Cox v. Rose, E.D.Tenn.1975, 386 F.Supp. 533.

Where not necessary to decision in habeas corpus case, hearing court would not consider constitutional question. Sluder v. Henderson, E.D.La.1971, 333 F.Supp. 401, affirmed 450 F.2d 351.

Federal habeas jurisdiction is limited to insuring that the state in enforcement of its criminal law fully accords state criminal defendants their federal constitutional rights; to inject a habeas court into substantive law upon which conviction rests would injure delicate relationship between federal and state governments. McGhee v. Sigler, D.C.Neb.1971, 328 F.Supp. 538, affirmed 455 F.2d 987, certiorari denied 93 S.Ct. 468, 409 U.S. 1022, 34 L.Ed.2d 314.

In habeas corpus proceeding by Louisiana defendant convicted under vagrancy statute on charge of loitering without being able to account for his lawful presence, inquiry into constitutionality of statute was limited to provisions penalizing persons loafing or loitering without lawful business or reason or persons unable to account for their lawful presence. Scott v. District Atty., Jefferson Parish, State of La., E.D.La.1970, 309 F.Supp. 833, affirmed 437 F.2d 500.

Findings to be Made by District Court

Where federal district court, although denying habeas corpus relief, stated that record raised serious questions about fundamental fairness of original state trial of petitioner and that there was evidence as to intimidation of his witnesses and racial prejudice in general in county at time of trial, district court would be required to make findings and conclusions of law relating thereto. Lee v. Beto, C.A.5 (Tex.) 1970, 429 F.2d 524.

Federal district court in habeas corpus proceeding by state prisoner should have made a finding on point raised by prisoner that he was deprived of adequate representation by counsel in state prosecution because counsel without objection permitted prior criminal record of prisoner to be introduced though character of prisoner had not been put in issue. Worts v. Dutton, C.A.5 (Ga.) 1968, 395 F.2d 341.

In making findings in a habeas proceeding, a judge must acknowledge significant portions of the record, particularly where they are inconsistent with the judge's findings; the process of explaining and reconciling seemingly inconsistent parts of the record lays bare the judicial thinking process, enabling a reviewing court to judge the rationality of the fact-finder's reasoning, and failure to take into account and reconcile key parts of the record casts doubt on the process by which the finding was reached, and hence on the correctness of the finding. Senteno v. California, E.D.Cal.2009, 705 F.Supp.2d 1175.

Procedural Bar Issues

Where neither state legislature nor state courts indicate that a federal constitutional claim is barred by some state procedural rule, a federal court implies no disrespect for the state by entertaining the claim in a habeas proceeding. County Court of Ulster County, N. Y. v. Allen, U.S.N.Y.1979, 99 S.Ct. 2213, 442 U.S. 140, 60 L.Ed.2d 777.

Federal habeas corpus jurisdiction is conferred by allegation of unconstitutional restraint and is not defeated by anything that may occur in state proceedings, and state procedural rules must yield to this overriding federal policy. Jackson v. Denno, U.S.N.Y.1964, 84 S.Ct. 1774, 378 U.S. 368, 12 L.Ed.2d 908, 28 O.O.2d 177. See, also, Labat v. Bennett, C.A. 5 (La.) 1966, 365 F.2d 698, certiorari denied 87 S.Ct. 1303, 386 U.S. 991, 18 L.Ed.2d 334.

A court on habeas corpus is bound by a state court's interpretation of its own procedural rule. Brewer v. Overberg, C.A.6 (Ohio) 1980, 624 F.2d 51, 19 O.O.3d 151, certiorari denied 101 S.Ct. 873, 449 U.S. 1085, 66 L.Ed.2d 810.

State Supreme Court's holding of waiver of all federal claims under state procedural law was not determinative in federal habeas corpus action brought by state prisoner. Rinehart v. Brewer, C.A.8 (Iowa) 1977, 561 F.2d 126.

Adequacy of state procedural bar, to serve as basis for procedural default on petition for federal habeas relief, is question of federal law. Garson v. Perlman, E.D.N.Y.2008, 541 F.Supp.2d 515.

It is a question of federal law for a federal court whether a state rule is sufficiently adequate and independent to bar federal review. Yarris v. Horn, E.D.Pa.2002, 230 F.Supp.2d 577.

District judge on habeas corpus may not defer to state court's findings of law but must apply applicable federal law to state court fact findings independently. Townsend v. Sain, U.S.Ill.1963, 83 S.Ct. 745, 372 U.S. 293, 9 L.Ed.2d 770.

Hearings on Habeas Petitions

Whether federal habeas petitioner has shown lack of diligence in failing to obtain evidentiary hearing in state court, for purposes of determining entitlement to evidentiary hearing on federal petition for habeas corpus, is question of federal law decided by federal habeas court. Boyle v. McKune, C.A.10 (Kan.) 2008, 544 F.3d 1132, certiorari denied 129 S.Ct. 1630, 556 U.S. 1136, 173 L.Ed.2d 1011.

Whether evidentiary hearing is required in habeas corpus action where petitioner is state prisoner is question of federal law. Dever v. Kansas State Penitentiary, C.A.10 (Kan.) 1994, 36 F.3d 1531.

Whether an evidentiary hearing is required in habeas corpus proceeding is a question of federal law; while erroneous denial of a state post-conviction evidentiary hearing may be relevant to determination of federal question, it is not dispositive. Toler v. Wyrick, C.A.8 (Mo.) 1977, 563 F.2d 372, certiorari denied 98 S.Ct. 1455, 435 U.S. 907, 55 L.Ed.2d 498.

Ineffective Assistance of Counsel Claims

Question of adequacy of representation afforded by state defendant's counsel, as a matter of current federal standards, is for a federal court in federal habeas corpus proceeding. Hegwood v. Swenson, W.D.Mo.1972, 344 F.Supp. 226.

All courts are required to apply federal standards in determining habeas corpus petitioner's claim of ineffective assistance of counsel and that his plea of guilty was not voluntarily tendered. Pedicord v. Swenson, W.D.Mo.1969, 304 F.Supp. 393, affirmed 431 F.2d 92.

Witnesses in State Court

When assessing a sufficiency of the evidence challenge to state conviction on a petition for a writ of habeas corpus, the court looks to state law only to establish the elements of the crime, and then turns to the federal question of whether the state court was objectively unreasonable in concluding that sufficient evidence supported its decision. Boyer v. Belleque, C.A.9 (Or.) 2011, 659 F.3d 957, certiorari denied 132 S.Ct. 2723, 566 U.S. 1039, 183 L.Ed.2d 78.

State court's interpretation of state evidentiary rule to require defense counsel to initiate and exhaust meaningful and independent efforts to locate witness, so as to prove witness' unavailability, as prerequisite to offering witness' testimony from prior related proceeding, was binding upon federal court in habeas corpus proceeding. Allen v. Morris, C.A.6 (Ohio) 1988, 845 F.2d 610, rehearing denied, certiorari denied 109 S.Ct. 799, 488 U.S. 1011, 102 L.Ed.2d 790.

Claim by petitioner convicted in New York state court for attempted predatory sexual assault, challenging the state court's denial of his request for the raw electronic data generated during DNA testing because it was not in possession or control of the state, was not cognizable on federal habeas review, as it involved a question of discovery governed by a New York statute. Beckham v. Miller, E.D.N.Y.2019, 366 F.Supp.3d 379, appeal dismissed 2019 WL 4061513.

In analyzing the sufficiency of the evidence at trial to support a conviction, a habeas court must look to state law to determine the elements of the crime. Cardona v. Goord, E.D.N.Y.2011, 811 F.Supp.2d 655.

Statements and Confessions in State Court

Federal district court was not required in proceeding on petition by state prisoner for federal habeas corpus relief to defer to dicta in state court opinion to effect that warnings given petitioner did not satisfy Miranda requirements. Evans v. Swenson, C.A.8 (Mo.) 1972, 455 F.2d 291, certiorari denied 92 S.Ct. 2508, 408 U.S. 929, 33 L.Ed.2d 342.

State court decision prescribing warnings to be given prior to obtaining confessions and admissions had no application in federal habeas corpus proceeding. Pendleton v. Nelson, C.A.9 (Cal.) 1968, 404 F.2d 1074.

In habeas corpus proceeding by state prisoner, presenting issue of voluntariness of confession which had been admitted without preliminary determination of voluntariness, State of New York would be required to prove voluntariness beyond reasonable doubt, in accordance with rule adopted in New York courts. U.S. ex rel. Castro v. LaVallee, S.D.N.Y.1968, 282 F.Supp. 718.

Harmless Error Determination by State Court

Any "harmless error" rule applied to violation, by state court, of provision of federal Constitution must be judged by federal standard. Wilson v. Anderson, C.A.9 (Cal.) 1967, 379 F.2d 330, reversed on other grounds 88 S.Ct. 1133, 390 U.S. 523, 20 L.Ed.2d 81, rehearing denied 88 S.Ct. 1812, 391 U.S. 929, 20 L.Ed.2d 670.

Habeas corpus court must apply federal standard of harmless error. Conyers v. Wainwright, S.D.Fla.1970, 309 F.Supp. 1101.

Remedies Under Habeas Corpus

District Court had jurisdiction to clarify that its order granting unconditional writ of habeas corpus did not bar retrial of state prisoner, since prisoner was still in custody on improperly obtained conviction when the court issued its initial order for release of prisoner, and the court, at that time, could have entered an order barring retrial. Girts v. Yanai, C.A.6 (Ohio) 2010, 600 F.3d 576, certiorari denied 131 S.Ct. 247, 562 U.S. 891, 178 L.Ed.2d 138.

Federal judge may, in his discretion, refuse to entertain petition for writ of habeas corpus should he believe that granting the writ will not significantly affect the position of the petitioner. van Geldern v. Field, C.A.9 (Cal.) 1974, 498 F.2d 400.

Habeas corpus will not lie to secure judicial decision which, even if determined in petitioner's favor, would not result in his immediate release. U.S. ex rel. DeVoney v. Pate, C.A.7 (Ill.) 1966, 359 F.2d 828, certiorari denied 87 S.Ct. 147, 385 U.S. 873, 17 L.Ed.2d 100.

Challenge that goes to constitutionality of physical confinement and seeks either immediate release from that confinement or shortening of its duration is appropriate habeas corpus action with its concomitant requirement of exhausting state remedies. McCray v. Dietz, D.C.N.J.1980, 517 F.Supp. 787.

Where plaintiff seeks neither release from custody nor redress of alleged civil rights violations incurred in his state criminal proceedings, relief by way of habeas corpus is inappropriate. Royster v. McGinnis, S.D.N.Y.1971, 332 F.Supp. 973, probable jurisdiction noted 92 S.Ct. 1247, 405 U.S. 986, 31 L.Ed.2d 452, reversed on other grounds 93 S.Ct. 1055, 410 U.S. 263, 35 L.Ed.2d 282.

Petition for habeas corpus should only be considered where immediate discharge will result, or where there is possibility of earlier discharge or parole. Kelly v. Wingo, W.D.Ky.1970, 313 F.Supp. 1059.

Only relief which can be given in habeas corpus proceeding is release from custody, and if all contentions made in application be sustained but it for some other reason retention of applicant in custody is lawful, then writ cannot be used. U.S. ex rel. Randazzo v. Follette, S.D.N.Y.1968, 282 F.Supp. 2, remanded 444 F.2d 625, certiorari denied 92 S.Ct. 232, 404 U.S. 916, 30 L.Ed.2d 191.

Relator in habeas corpus proceeding must be in custody because of sentence he attacks, and for writ to be available, prisoner must be entitled to his immediate release. U.S. ex rel. Watson v. Myers, E.D.Pa.1966, 250 F.Supp. 292.

Exhaustion of Claims in State Court and Procedural Bar

When federal habeas corpus petition by state prisoner raises new constitutional issue, state law must be examined to determine utility of requiring exhaustion of state remedies. Whippler v. Balkcom, C.A.5 (Ga.) 1965, 342 F.2d 388. See, also, Smart v. Balkcom, C.A. 5 (Ga.) 1965, 352 F.2d 502.

Issue of whether state prisoner who had not appealed from denial of his state post-conviction relief application had thereby finally litigated his claim so as to have exhausted his state remedies was question to be decided by state courts. U.S. ex rel. Bowen v. Mazurkiewicz, E.D.Pa.1970, 309 F.Supp. 2, rehearing denied 315 F.Supp. 789.

Whether a state remedy is presently available to a habeas petitioner is a question of state law as to which only state courts may speak with final authority. Thomas v. Wyrick, C.A.8 (Mo.) 1980, 622 F.2d 411, on remand 520 F.Supp. 139.

Federal habeas corpus statute requires that state prisoners first seek redress in state forum, before bringing federal habeas corpus action. Heck v. Humphrey, U.S.Ind.1994, 114 S.Ct. 2364, 512 U.S. 477, 129 L.Ed.2d 383.

Exhaustion of remedies doctrine cannot be used to shatter attempt at litigation of constitutional claims without regard to purposes that underlie doctrine and that called it into existence. Braden v. 30th Judicial Circuit Court of Kentucky, U.S.Ky.1973, 93 S.Ct. 1123, 410 U.S. 484, 35 L.Ed.2d 443.

To satisfy exhaustion requirement, habeas petitioner must have fairly presented claim in state courts in order to give them opportunity to pass upon and correct alleged violation of his rights. Rose v. Palmateer, C.A.9 (Or.) 2005, 395 F.3d 1108, certiorari denied 125 S.Ct. 2971, 545 U.S. 1144, 162 L.Ed.2d 896.

Exhaustion of all claims does not bar federal courthouse door to any habeas corpus petitioner. (Per Tjoflat, Circuit Judge, with six Judges concurring and one Judge specially concurring.) Galtieri v. Wainwright, C.A.5 (Fla.) 1978, 582 F.2d 348, rehearing denied 587 F.2d 508.

Exhaustion requirement of this section is not an inflexible requirement. Rice v. Wolff, C.A.8 (Neb.) 1975, 513 F.2d 1280, certiorari granted 95 S.Ct. 2677, 422 U.S. 1055, 45 L.Ed.2d 707, reversed on other grounds 96 S.Ct. 3037, 428 U.S. 465, 49 L.Ed.2d 1067, on remand 539 F.2d 693, rehearing denied 97 S.Ct. 197, 429 U.S. 874, 50 L.Ed.2d 158. See, also, Green v. Wyrick, D.C.Mo.1976, 414 F.Supp. 343, affirmed 542 F.2d 1178.

The exhaustion doctrine should not be applied mechanically without regard to factual setting in habeas corpus proceeding in federal court by state prisoner. Pate v. Holman, C.A.5 (Ala.) 1965, 343 F.2d 546.

Orderly and reasonable state procedures should be exhausted before state prisoner's habeas corpus petition will be entertained in federal court. Hunt v. Warden, Md. Penitentiary, C.A.4 (Md.) 1964, 335 F.2d 936.

Absent exceptional circumstances, a federal court cannot review a state prisoner's habeas application on the merits unless the petitioner has exhausted his remedies under state law. Flowers v. Morgan, D.Del.2013, 940 F.Supp.2d 136, subsequent determination 945 F.Supp.2d 540.

Federal courts may not grant a writ of habeas corpus to a state petitioner unless petitioner has exhausted the remedies available in state courts, or there is either an absence of available state corrective process or the existence of circumstances rendering such process ineffective to protect the rights of prisoners. Copeland v. Walker, E.D.N.Y.2003, 258 F.Supp.2d 105.

Federal courts must conduct a four-step analysis to determine whether habeas corpus petition may be considered when its claims have not been presented to a state court: first step is to determine if petitioner fairly presented the federal constitutional dimensions of his federal habeas corpus claim to state courts, second step requires that federal court determine whether petitioner has exhausted his state remedies, or if any existing state remedies are futile, third step is to determine whether petitioner has demonstrated adequate cause to excuse his failure to raise the claim in state court and the final step is to determine whether failure to address the merits of the petitioner's claim in state court would result in actual prejudice. Fairchild v. Lockhart, E.D.Ark.1989, 744 F.Supp. 1429, affirmed 900 F.2d 1292, rehearing denied, certiorari denied 111 S.Ct. 21, 497 U.S. 1052, 111 L.Ed.2d 834.

"Shotgun" approach followed by petitioner for writ of habeas corpus in filing numerous pleadings among different state and federal courts did not constitute compliance with mandate of exhaustion under this section. McClain v. Duckworth, N.D.Ind.1983, 569 F.Supp. 840.

The exhaustion requirement is part of the common law heritage which applies to all habeas statutes. U.S. ex rel. Scranton v. State of New York, S.D.N.Y.1975, 402 F.Supp. 1010, affirmed 532 F.2d 292.

Exhaustion doctrine requires exhaustion of remedies rather than exhaustion of petitioner. Emmett v. Ricketts, N.D.Ga.1975, 397 F.Supp. 1025.

At the least, exhaustion of remedies requires that the petitioner attempt to do for himself that which he asks the habeas corpus court to do for him. Gilstrap v. Godwin, E.D.Va.1974, 383 F.Supp. 1013.

Exhaustion of state remedy rule should ordinarily be strictly adhered to before federal court accepts habeas corpus jurisdiction. Renfro v. Swenson, W.D.Mo.1970, 315 F.Supp. 733.

Exhaustion requirement of this section is merely an accommodation of federal system designed to give state an initial opportunity to pass on and correct alleged violations of its prisoners' federal rights. Wilwording v. Swenson, U.S.Mo.1971, 92 S.Ct. 407, 404 U.S. 249, 30 L.Ed.2d 418. See, also, Ray v. Howard, E.D.Pa.1980, 486 F.Supp. 638; Canfora v. Davenport, D.C.N.J.1972, 350 F.Supp. 1020.

It is appropriate to address merits of habeas corpus petition notwithstanding failure to exhaust available state remedies, if interests of comity and federalism will be better served by addressing merits forthwith; if Court of Appeals is convinced that petition has no merit, belated application of exhaustion rule might simply require useless litigation in state courts. Hoxsie v. Kerby, C.A.10 (N.M.) 1997, 108 F.3d 1239, certiorari denied 118 S.Ct. 126, 522 U.S. 844, 139 L.Ed.2d 77.

Habeas petitioner's unexhausted claim that his due process rights were violated when his vacated guilty plea was revealed to the jury was colorable, and thus claim could not be denied on the merits by federal habeas court until state court had the opportunity to consider it. Cassett v. Stewart, C.A.9 (Ariz.) 2005, 406 F.3d 614, certiorari denied 126 S.Ct. 1336, 546 U.S. 1172, 164 L.Ed.2d 52.

Once a federal claim has been fairly presented at the first possible opportunity within one complete round of a state's established appellate review process, the claim has been exhausted for purposes of federal habeas review. Carter v. Mitchell, C.A.6 (Ohio) 2012, 693 F.3d 555, on remand 2013 WL 146366.

When the state court articulates its reasons for rejecting a federal claim on its merits, habeas court reviews those reasons; when a state court fails to articulate the rationale underlying its rejection of a federal claim, however, habeas review focuses on the state court's ultimate decision. Jimenez v. Walker, C.A.2 (N.Y.) 2006, 458 F.3d 130, certiorari denied 127 S.Ct. 976, 549 U.S. 1133, 166 L.Ed.2d 740.

A complete round of the state appellate process, as required to meet federal habeas statute's exhaustion requirement, includes discretionary appellate review when that review is part of the ordinary appellate review procedure in the State. Dill v. Holt, C.A.11 (Ala.) 2004, 371 F.3d 1301.

Absent compliance with exhaustion requirements of this section, it ordinarily is inappropriate for a federal court to entertain a state prisoner's petition for a writ of habeas corpus. U.S. ex rel. Johnson v. Vincent, C.A.2 (N.Y.) 1974, 507 F.2d 1309, certiorari denied 95 S.Ct. 1435, 420 U.S. 994, 43 L.Ed.2d 678. See, also, U.S. ex rel. Brodie v. Hilton, D.C.N.J.1980, 496 F.Supp. 619.

A New York inmate challenging denial of his parole exhausts his available remedies, for purposes of seeking federal habeas relief, by filing an appeal with the appeals unit, petitioning state court for Article 78 relief, and appealing a denial of Article 78 relief to the highest state court capable of reviewing it. Siao-Pao v. Connolly, S.D.N.Y.2008, 564 F.Supp.2d 232.

Federal court may not consider a petition for a writ of habeas corpus unless the petitioner has exhausted all state judicial remedies. Pitter v. Fischer, S.D.N.Y.2002, 234 F.Supp.2d 342.

Exhaustion of state remedies is required as a prerequisite to consideration of each claim sought to be presented by a state prisoner in a federal habeas corpus proceeding. Pitchess v. Davis, U.S.Cal.1975, 95 S.Ct. 1748, 421 U.S. 482, 44 L.Ed.2d 317. See, also, Manning v. State of Ala., C.A. 5 (Ala.) 1976, 526 F.2d 355.

Exhaustion of state remedies is required as prerequisite to consideration of each claim sought to be presented in federal habeas, and it is not enough that state has been presented with general factual background of petitioner's case or legal contentions related to that presently urged, but, rather, state prisoner is required to first present to state courts the "same claim" that he urges upon federal court before he may properly seek relief in that latter forum. Grace v. Butterworth, C.A.1 (Mass.) 1980, 635 F.2d 1, certiorari denied 101 S.Ct. 3053, 452 U.S. 917, 69 L.Ed.2d 421.

State prison inmate's habeas claim for ineffective assistance of trial counsel, in request for certificate of appealability (COA) with respect to district court's denial of federal habeas relief, were neither presented in federal habeas petition nor exhausted in state court, and thus inmate failed to meet requirements for federal review of claims pursuant to Antiterrorism and Effective Death Penalty Act (AEDPA); claim appeared nowhere in habeas petition, which alleged ineffective assistance of appellate counsel, and inmate never presented claim for ineffective assistance of trial counsel for review by state courts. Milton v. Miller, C.A.10 (Okla.) 2016, 812 F.3d 1252, certiorari denied 137 S.Ct. 69, 196 L.Ed.2d 65.

State prisoner espoused same legal theory throughout his state proceedings, as required under Antiterrorism and Effective Death Penalty Act (AEDPA) to exhaust his administrative remedies so that federal court could consider his Batson claim; although exact wording of prisoner's arguments may have varied over time, prisoner made only one Batson objection at trial and he argued to each state court that government's challenge of particular juror was improper because based upon juror's race. Sanchez v. Roden, C.A.1 (Mass.) 2014, 753 F.3d 279.

When a federal habeas petition raises a claim that has not been exhausted in state proceedings, the district court ordinarily must either dismiss the petition, leaving the prisoner with the choice of returning to state court to exhaust his claims, or of amending or resubmitting the habeas petition to present only exhausted claims to the district court, or grant a stay and abeyance to allow the petitioner to exhaust the unexhausted claim. Ogle v. Johnson, C.A.11 (Ga.) 2007, 488 F.3d 1364, on remand 2008 WL 6493628.

State inmate's failure to exhaust his state court remedies barred his emergency petition for writ of habeas corpus alleging that denial of bail pending state trial court's reconsideration of his sentence violated his due process rights, notwithstanding approximately two-month COVID-19-related deferral of adjudication of his state court motions. Malloy v. District Attorney of Montgomery County, E.D.Pa.2020, 461 F.Supp.3d 168.

As a general rule, federal courts should deny writs of habeas corpus to obtain release from custody pursuant to judgment of a state court, if state corrective process is available, but such rule is not rigid and inflexible and district courts may deviate from it and grant relief in special circumstances. Frisbie v. Collins, U.S.Mich.1952, 72 S.Ct. 509, 342 U.S. 519, 96 L.Ed. 541, rehearing denied 72 S.Ct. 768, 343 U.S. 937, 96 L.Ed. 1344. See, also, Bacom v. Sullivan, C.A.Fla.1952, 194 F.2d 166.

Courts may grant habeas corpus in special circumstances, even though petitioner did not exhaust state remedies. Chitwood v. Dowd, C.A.8 (Mo.) 1989, 889 F.2d 781, rehearing denied, certiorari denied 110 S.Ct. 2219, 495 U.S. 953, 109 L.Ed.2d 545.

Federal courts may deviate from habeas exhaustion requirement only where highly exceptional circumstances warrant prompt federal intervention. Jones v. Solem, C.A.8 (S.D.) 1984, 739 F.2d 329.

Oklahoma's use of laches doctrine to bar applications for postconviction relief brought after decades had elapsed since trial was independent and adequate state procedural bar that could be applied functionally to exhaust claims brought in federal habeas through anticipatory procedural default, and thus petitioner's claim that state violated his right to counsel based on interference with attorney-client relationship, based on evidence discovered more than 30 years after his conviction, would be anticipatorily barred on procedural ground of laches, and, as result, was procedurally defaulted and exhausted for purposes of federal habeas review. Fontenot v. Crow, C.A.10 (Okla.) 2021, 4 F.4th 982.

Federal court was barred from reviewing state prisoner's claims that his due process rights were violated, that his right to a fair trial was violated, and that the evidence against him was legally insufficient to support his conviction for rape, on prisoner's petition for federal habeas relief, where prisoner defaulted on such claims by not exhausting them before state appellate court, prisoner did not allege cause and prejudice for his default, and prisoner did not raise a claim of actual innocence. Pham v. Kirkpatrick, N.D.N.Y.2016, 209 F.Supp.3d 497, affirmed 711 Fed.Appx. 67, 2018 WL 921540, certiorari denied 138 S.Ct. 2585, 201 L.Ed.2d 302.

Federal habeas petitioner's failure to exhaust state remedies will be excused if state procedural rules preclude him from seeking further relief in state courts; although treated as technically exhausted, such claims are nonetheless procedurally defaulted. Price v. Phelps, D.Del.2012, 894 F.Supp.2d 504.

Although district court was required to excuse petitioner's failure to exhaust state remedies for her federal habeas claims as to which, under state-court rules, petitioner was barred from obtaining further review in state courts, claims were still procedurally defaulted, precluding district court's review of their merits absent showing of cause and prejudice or that miscarriage of justice would occur absent review. Drummond v. Ryan, D.Del.2008, 572 F.Supp.2d 528.

Petitioner exhausted his claim that he was denied effective assistance of counsel as result of counsel's failure to object to trial court's defective plea procedure, where petitioner's initial pro se brief in state post-conviction proceeding explained what procedure state law required before his proffered plea of guilty but mentally ill (GBMI) could be accepted, then explained that counsel was deficient for failing to object to trial judge's failure to apply those procedures. Velazquez v. Superintendent Fayette SCI, C.A.3 (Pa.) 2019, 937 F.3d 151.

Federal habeas statute's exhaustion requirement is not jurisdictional prerequisite and, as result, may be waived by state. Divers v. Cain, C.A.5 (La.) 2012, 698 F.3d 211, certiorari denied 133 S.Ct. 1806, 569 U.S. 926, 185 L.Ed.2d 826.

A finding of waiver by a state postconviction court is enough to establish an adequate and independent state ground for dismissing a claim, such that a federal court reviewing a petition for a writ of habeas corpus by a petitioner seeking relief from the state-court conviction will not review the claim even if it presents a question of federal law. Sturgeon v. Chandler, C.A.7 (Ill.) 2009, 552 F.3d 604, rehearing and rehearing en banc denied.

Petitioner was not barred from seeking collateral review of his unexhausted federal constitutional claim under Arizona law, although he was represented by counsel on appeal in state court; petitioner instructed his court-appointed appellate counsel to raise his federal constitutional claim in his direct appeal and his attorney believed that he had raised issue in briefs filed on his client's behalf. Johnson v. Lewis, C.A.9 (Ariz.) 1991, 929 F.2d 460.

Requiring exhaustion before allowing state prisoners access to federal courts to attack validity of fact or length of their confinement means that prisoner's state remedy must be adequate and available. Preiser v. Rodriguez, U.S.N.Y.1973, 93 S.Ct. 1827, 411 U.S. 475, 36 L.Ed.2d 439.

An applicant for habeas corpus in federal court shall not be deemed to have exhausted remedies available in courts of the state within meaning of this section, if he has right under state law to raise, by any available procedure, the question presented. U.S. ex rel. Auld v. Warden of N.J. State Penitentiary, C.A.3 (N.J.) 1951, 187 F.2d 615. See, also, Ames v. Middlebrooks, C.A.5 (La.) 1966, 369 F.2d 113, certiorari denied 87 S.Ct. 1050, 386 U.S. 967, 18 L.Ed.2d 119; U.S. ex rel. Rivera v. LaVallee, C.A.2 (N.Y.) 1963, 319 F.2d 849; Saulsbury v. Green, C.A.6 (Ohio) 1963, 318 F.2d 320; Kramer v. State of Nevada, C.C.A.Nev.1941, 122 F.2d 417; Johnson v. Wyrick, D.C.Mo.1974, 381 F.Supp. 747, affirmed 508 F.2d 123; Donovan v. Delgado, D.C.Puerto Rico, 1971, 339 F.Supp. 446; Huffman v. Tollett, D.C.Tenn.1970, 321 F.Supp. 58; King v. Cook, D.C.Miss.1968, 287 F.Supp. 269; White v. Swenson, D.C.Mo.1966, 261 F.Supp. 42; Miller v. Boles, D.C.W.Va.1965, 248 F.Supp. 49.

Threshold question in all federal habeas corpus cases is whether or not federal habeas applicant has first exhausted his available state remedies before turning to federal courts to seek relief. Ryan v. State of La., E.D.La.1970, 314 F.Supp. 1047, affirmed 433 F.2d 996. See, also, McInnes v. Anderson, D.C.Okl.1973, 366 F.Supp. 983.

Federal court's disposition of state prisoner's petition for habeas corpus must be consistent with principles of exhaustion of available state corrective process. Donnell v. Swenson, W.D.Mo.1969, 302 F.Supp. 1024.

Habeas corpus requirement that petitioner must have exhausted all state court remedies available absent certain circumstances is strictly enforced, in interests of giving state courts first opportunity to consider and, if necessary, correct alleged constitutional errors in conviction and sentencing. Pruett v. Thompson, E.D.Va.1991, 771 F.Supp. 1428, affirmed 996 F.2d 1560, certiorari denied 114 S.Ct. 487, 510 U.S. 984, 126 L.Ed.2d 437, rehearing denied 114 S.Ct. 652, 510 U.S. 1032, 126 L.Ed.2d 609.

It is national policy that in the district court's exercise of its power to entertain and dispose of petitions for habeas corpus, it shall not grant affirmative relief to a state prisoner until he has exhausted the remedies available in the state courts. U.S. ex rel. Drew v. Myers, C.A.3 (Pa.) 1964, 327 F.2d 174, certiorari denied 85 S.Ct. 88, 379 U.S. 847, 13 L.Ed.2d 52.

It is incumbent on federal courts to ascertain whether states afford an available remedy which has not yet been exhausted to correct an abuse of due process in administration of their criminal laws. U.S. ex rel. Wilkins v. Banmiller, C.A.3 (Pa.) 1963, 325 F.2d 514, certiorari denied 85 S.Ct. 87, 379 U.S. 847, 13 L.Ed.2d 51. See, also, Manning v. State of Ala., C.A.5 (Ala.) 1976, 526 F.2d 355.

Federal district court in habeas corpus proceeding must make independent determination of whether petitioner had exhausted state remedies still available to him. Peters v. Dillon, D.C.Colo.1964, 227 F.Supp. 487.

Because requirement that habeas corpus applicants exhaust remedies available in state court refers only to remedies still available at time of federal habeas petition, requirement is satisfied if it is clear that habeas petitioner's claims are now procedurally barred under state law. Gray v. Netherland, U.S.Va.1996, 116 S.Ct. 2074, 518 U.S. 152, 135 L.Ed.2d 457, rehearing denied 117 S.Ct. 22, 518 U.S. 1047, 135 L.Ed.2d 1116, on remand 99 F.3d 158.

Where resort to state court remedies has failed to afford full and fair adjudication of federal contentions raised by one detained under state court judgment of conviction, either because state affords no remedy or because in particular case remedy afforded by state law proves in practice unavailable or seriously inadequate, a federal court should entertain petition for habeas corpus, but in such case petitioner should proceed in federal district court before resorting to United State Supreme Court. Ex parte Hawk, U.S.Neb.1944, 64 S.Ct. 448, 321 U.S. 114, 88 L.Ed. 572.

A conviction that rests upon a defendant's state law "procedural default" (for example, the defendant's failure to raise a claim of error at the time or in the place that state law requires), normally rests upon an independent and adequate state ground; and where a conviction rests upon such a ground, a federal habeas court normally cannot consider the defendant's federal constitutional claim. Trevino v. Thaler, U.S.2013, 133 S.Ct. 1911, 569 U.S. 413, 185 L.Ed.2d 1044, on remand 740 F.3d 378.

Under the doctrine of "procedural default," a federal habeas court will not review the merits of claims, including constitutional claims, that a state court declined to hear because the prisoner failed to abide by a state procedural rule. Martinez v. Ryan, U.S.2012, 132 S.Ct. 1309, 566 U.S. 1, 182 L.Ed.2d 272, on remand 680 F.3d 1160.

As a rule, a state prisoner's habeas claims may not be entertained by a federal court when: (1) a state court has declined to address those claims because the prisoner had failed to meet a state procedural requirement, and (2) the state judgment rests on independent and adequate state procedural grounds. Maples v. Thomas, U.S.2012, 132 S.Ct. 912, 565 U.S. 266, 181 L.Ed.2d 807, on remand 460 Fed.Appx. 860, 2012 WL 752467.

Not every state procedural default bars federal habeas corpus relief. Humphrey v. Cady, U.S.Wis.1972, 92 S.Ct. 1048, 405 U.S. 504, 31 L.Ed.2d 394.

Whether a state procedural rule serves as an independent and adequate ground on which the state can rely to foreclose review of a federal constitutional claim, so as to preclude federal habeas review, is a question to be answered by the federal courts. Clifton v. Carpenter, C.A.6 (Tenn.) 2014, 775 F.3d 760, on remand 2016 WL 918049.

Petitioner's federal claims were procedurally defaulted upon his petition for federal habeas corpus review, where state appellate court's determination that federal claims were defaulted on state motion for relief from judgment was based on independent and adequate state procedural rule prohibiting state court from granting such relief if petitioner could have raised claims on appeal or in prior motion for relief from judgment, absent good cause for failure and actual prejudice. Burroughs v. Makowski, C.A.6 (Mich.) 2002, 282 F.3d 410, modified on rehearing 35 Fed.Appx. 402, 2002 WL 1115469.

For purposes of habeas corpus relief proceedings, "procedural default doctrine" is specific application of general adequate and independent state grounds doctrine. Calderon v. U.S. Dist. Court for Eastern Dist. of California, C.A.9 (Cal.) 1996, 96 F.3d 1126, certiorari denied 117 S.Ct. 1569, 520 U.S. 1204, 137 L.Ed.2d 714.

When state remedies are rendered unavailable by petitioner's own procedural default, federal courts are barred from reviewing those claims. Sones v. Hargett, C.A.5 (Miss.) 1995, 61 F.3d 410.

Generally, "procedural default" in habeas corpus case occurs when defendant has failed to press constitutional challenge to his conviction to highest state court, thereby failing to accord state courts full opportunity to correct any constitutional errors. Mills v. Jordan, C A.7 (Ind.) 1992, 979 F.2d 1273.

If no state remedy is available for unexhausted habeas claim, then claim is considered procedurally defaulted, and cannot serve as grounds for federal habeas corpus relief unless petitioner can demonstrate cause and prejudice. Whitepipe v. Weber, D.S.D.2007, 536 F.Supp.2d 1070.

Where a state court rejects a petitioner's claim because the petitioner failed to comply with a state procedural rule, the procedural default constitutes an adequate and independent ground for the state court decision; a procedural default will bar federal habeas review of the federal claim, unless the habeas petitioner can show cause for the default and prejudice attributable thereto or demonstrate that failure to consider the federal claim will result in a fundamental miscarriage of justice. Rolling v. Fischer, S.D.N.Y.2006, 433 F.Supp.2d 336.

Grounds to Issue Writ

In conducting habeas review, a federal court is limited to deciding whether a conviction violated the Constitution, laws, or treaties of the United States. Middleton v. Roper, C.A.8 (Mo.) 2006, 455 F.3d 838, certiorari denied 127 S.Ct. 980, 549 U.S. 1134, 166 L.Ed.2d 743.

If federal court is in grave doubt about whether trial error had substantial and injurious effect or influence on verdict and therefore finds itself in virtual equipoise about such issue, error is not harmless, and habeas corpus relief would be warranted. Cooper v. Taylor, C.A.4 (S.C.) 1996, 103 F.3d 366, certiorari denied 118 S.Ct. 83, 522 U.S. 824, 139 L.Ed.2d 40.

Even if a state petitioner does not waive a ground for habeas corpus relief by failure to raise ground in state proceedings, a federal redetermination is not automatic. Vera v. Beto, S.D.Tex.1971, 332 F.Supp. 1197.

In order for habeas corpus relief to be granted, conviction sought to be set aside must be predicated to some degree on matters alleged as grounds for relief. Henderson v. Beto, N.D.Tex.1970, 309 F.Supp. 244.

In general, if a convicted state criminal defendant can show a federal habeas court that his conviction rests upon a violation of the Federal Constitution, he may well obtain a writ of habeas corpus that requires a new trial, a new sentence, or release. Trevino v. Thaler, U.S.2013, 133 S.Ct. 1911, 569 U.S. 413, 185 L.Ed.2d 1044, on remand 740 F.3d 378.

A state prisoner seeking federal habeas corpus relief must prove that some constitutional infirmity occurred in proceedings resulting in conviction. Tollett v. Henderson, U.S.Tenn.1973, 93 S.Ct. 1602, 411 U.S. 258, 36 L.Ed.2d 235.

Remedy of federal habeas corpus is freely available to state defendants if at trial they are in fact denied any federal constitutional rights and these denials go uncorrected by other courts of state. City of Greenwood, Miss. v. Peacock, U.S.Miss.1966, 86 S.Ct. 1800, 384 U.S. 808, 16 L.Ed.2d 944.

Habeas petition drew enough of a connection between petitioner's right to due process and the trial court's alleged evidentiary and instructional errors to render petitioner's claim cognizable on habeas review; petitioner articulated the theory of self-defense that he wished to pursue, described the evidence both excluded and admitted that supported that theory, and argued that preventing him from pursuing the theory of self-defense likely resulted in the conviction of an innocent person. Perruquet v. Briley, C.A.7 (Ill.) 2004, 390 F.3d 505.

In reviewing state prosecutor's conduct in habeas corpus action, court of appeals is precluded from applying broad supervisory powers available on direct review; rather, habeas corpus relief is available only when state has violated some right protected by U.S.C.A. Const. Amend. 14. Runnels v. Hess, C.A.10 (Okla.) 1981, 653 F.2d 1359.

Scope of federal court's review of a state court proceeding is “the narrow one of due process,” and not every trial error or infirmity which might call for application of supervisory powers correspondingly constitutes a “failure to observe that fundamental fairness essential to the very concept of justice.” Borodine v. Douzanis, C.A.1 (Mass.) 1979, 592 F.2d 1202.

Errors of state trial court are not reviewable on federal habeas corpus unless there has been a deprivation of constitutional rights such as to render judgment void or to amount to denial of due process. Scalf v. Bennett, C.A.8 (Iowa) 1969, 408 F.2d 325, certiorari denied 90 S.Ct. 175, 396 U.S. 887, 24 L.Ed.2d 161.

When denial of due process resulting in unlawful detention is not shown, a federal court lacks jurisdiction to grant habeas corpus relief to a state prisoner. Robinson v. Wainwright, C.A.5 (Fla.) 1967, 387 F.2d 438.

Federal habeas corpus is available for purpose of making an inquiry as to whether particular state prosecution offends due process clause of U.S.C.A.Const. Amend. 14, and of affording relief if a violation of such clause is found. Barnett v. Gladden, C.A.9 (Or.) 1967, 375 F.2d 235.

"Actual innocence" is not itself a constitutional claim, for purposes of federal habeas review. Ortiz v. Barkley, S.D.N.Y.2008, 558 F.Supp.2d 444.

Claim that cumulative effect of errors rendered state-court trial fundamentally unfair is not cognizable on federal habeas petition. Sheppard v. Bagley, C.A.6 (Ohio) 2011, 657 F.3d 338, rehearing and rehearing en banc denied, certiorari denied 132 S.Ct. 2751, 567 U.S. 910, 183 L.Ed.2d 623.

In federal habeas context, cumulative error analysis, which aggregates all errors found to be harmless and analyzes whether their cumulative effect on outcome of trial is such that collectively they can no longer be determined to be harmless, applies only to cumulative constitutional errors. Young v. Sirmons, C.A.10 (Okla.) 2008, 551 F.3d 942, certiorari denied 130 S.Ct. 272, 558 U.S. 906, 175 L.Ed.2d 183.

Right to Assistance of Counsel

Since a defense attorney's representation of conflicting interests makes the trial fundamentally unfair, such a trial violates due process and no other state action need be shown. Zuck v. State of Ala., C.A.5 (Ala.) 1979, 588 F.2d 436, rehearing denied 591 F.2d 102, certiorari denied 100 S.Ct. 63, 444 U.S. 833, 62 L.Ed.2d 42.

Failure of either court-appointed counsel, seeking to terminate attorney-client relationship with prisoner following affirmance of his conviction by Florida District Court of Appeals, or public defender, requested by prisoner to obtain review by Florida Supreme Court by certiorari, or both to make timely petition for certiorari was sufficient state action to authorize federal habeas corpus relief with respect to state prisoner. Pressley v. Wainwright, C.A.5 (Fla.) 1976, 540 F.2d 818, rehearing denied 543 F.2d 756, certiorari denied 97 S.Ct. 1688, 430 U.S. 987, 52 L.Ed.2d 383.

State prisoner whose privately retained attorney did not request court reporter for criminal proceedings, apparently to diminish his client's expenses, and who asserted that nonexistence of trial transcript precluded effective appeal failed to demonstrate state involvement which is requisite to relief under this section. Morgan v. Massey, C.A.5 (Fla.) 1976, 526 F.2d 347, certiorari denied 97 S.Ct. 533, 429 U.S. 1002, 50 L.Ed.2d 613.

Requisite state action for federal habeas corpus purposes was present where Assistant State Attorney was actively involved in creating the conflict of interest with respect to retained attorney who, representing both habeas corpus petitioner and one of his codefendants in state trial, recommended that petitioner not accept plea bargain offer on ground that petitioner's testimony would injure codefendant who was also attorney's client. Alvarez v. Wainwright, C.A.5 (Fla.) 1975, 522 F.2d 100.

If incompetency of a retained attorney's representation is so apparent that a reasonably attentive official of state should have been aware of and could have corrected it, state action requirement for federal habeas corpus purposes is satisfied. Fitzgerald v. Estelle, C.A.5 (Tex.) 1974, 505 F.2d 1334, certiorari denied 95 S.Ct. 2636, 422 U.S. 1011, 45 L.Ed.2d 675. See, also, Alvarez v. Wainwright, C.A. 5 (Fla.) 1975, 522 F.2d 100.

Where public defender was appointed to represent accused for purposes of appeal and several weeks yet remained for timely filing of notice of direct appeal but instead public defender waited and filed an untimely appeal of denial of accused's motion for postconviction relief, failure to act constituted state action which effectively denied to accused his constitutionally protected right to appeal. Hall v. Wainwright, C.A.5 (Fla.) 1971, 441 F.2d 391.

For petitioner to be entitled to postconviction relief, it is not enough to show that indigency occasioned his inability to employ counsel or to appeal; petitioner must show that state deprived him of his rights under

U.S.C.A.Const. Amend. 14; state action is shown when responsible official in state's system of justice rejects a request for counsel or fails to take proper steps toward appointment of counsel for convicted defendant when official has knowledge of defendant's indigency and desire for appellate counsel. McGriff v. Wainwright, C.A.5 (Fla.) 1970, 431 F.2d 897. See, also, Loter v. Estelle, C.A. 5 (Tex.) 1977, 546 F.2d 151, certiorari denied 98 S.Ct. 150, 434 U.S. 846, 54 L.Ed.2d 112.

Conviction of petitioner under such grossly unfair circumstances as to cast doubt upon factual basis upon which proof of guilt rests is sufficient state action to invoke constitutional protections, though such unfairness arose from actions of retained, rather than appointed, counsel. Wilson v. Phend, C.A.7 (Ind.) 1969, 417 F.2d 1197.

Alleged misrepresentation of retained counsel concerning only admissibility of evidence in state court's prosecution was not such “state action” as would entitle state prisoner to habeas corpus relief under U.S.C.A.Const. Amend. 14. Johnson v. Smith, C.A.5 (Ga.) 1969, 414 F.2d 645, certiorari denied 90 S.Ct. 975, 397 U.S. 951, 25 L.Ed.2d 133.

Denial of right to have effective assistance of competent counsel in prosecution in state court opens judgment of conviction to challenge by state prisoner in habeas corpus proceeding in federal district court, but lack of effective assistance of competent counsel in state prosecution does not, since alleged incompetence of attorney of state prisoner cannot be imputed to the state. Howard v. Beto, C.A.5 (Tex.) 1967, 375 F.2d 441.

Mistake of counsel in failing to perfect an appeal from conviction, while regrettable, did not constitute a denial of due process, and did not entitle client to habeas corpus where error did not occur because of any action by state. King v. Wainwright, C.A.5 (Fla.) 1966, 368 F.2d 57, certiorari denied 88 S.Ct. 499, 389 U.S. 995, 19 L.Ed.2d 492.

Even where defendant has been represented by a retained attorney at trial, if at appeal stage he is without funds but desires to appeal and makes such desire known, failure to inform him of his right to appointment of counsel is ground for habeas corpus relief. Reynolds v. Lockhart, C.A.8 (Ark.) 1974, 497 F.2d 314.

Ineffective Assistance of Counsel

Federal court may grant habeas relief on “ineffective assistance” grounds, though state court has already rejected “ineffective assistance” claim, if state court's decision was contrary to, or involved unreasonable application of, clearly established federal law, as determined by the United States Supreme Court. Yarborough v. Gentry, U.S.2003, 124 S.Ct. 1, 540 U.S. 1, 157 L.Ed.2d 1, on remand 381 F.3d 1219.

Court of Appeals would review habeas petitioner's Strickland claim through lens of statutory provision which permits a federal court to issue a writ of habeas corpus only if the state court reached a decision that was contrary to, or involved an unreasonable application of, clearly established Federal law as determined by the Supreme Court, where petitioner sought relief from state conviction. Brady v. Pfister, C.A.7 (Ill.) 2013, 711 F.3d 818.

When a state court adjudicates a petitioner's ineffective assistance of counsel claim on the merits, a federal court can issue a writ of habeas corpus only if the state court's decision was either contrary to, or involved an unreasonable application of clearly established federal law, as determined by the Supreme Court of the United States, or was based on an unreasonable determination of the facts in light of the evidence presented in the State court proceeding; the state court's application of federal law must not only be incorrect, but objectively unreasonable, which typically involves the state court applying a rule different from the governing law set forth in Supreme Court cases, or deciding a case differently than the Supreme Court on a set of materially indistinguishable facts. Rann v. Atchison, C.A.7 (Ill.) 2012, 689 F.3d 832, certiorari denied 133 S.Ct. 672, 568 U.S. 1030, 184 L.Ed.2d 464.

For ineffective assistance claim previously rejected by state courts to provide basis for federal habeas relief, it is not enough for habeas petitioner to convince federal habeas court that, in its independent judgment, state court applied Strickland incorrectly; rather, he must show that state court applied Strickland to facts of his case in objectively unreasonable manner. Cox v. Donnelly, C.A.2 (N.Y.) 2004, 387 F.3d 193, on remand 2004 WL 2786311.

Federal habeas petitioner was not entitled to relief on grounds that state court's rejection of his ineffective assistance of counsel claim was contrary to established United States Supreme Court precedent, inasmuch as state court correctly applied Strickland standard for claims of ineffective assistance of counsel, which was clearly established federal law, and Supreme Court had not addressed facts materially indistinguishable from those in petitioner's case. Roche v. Davis, C.A.7 (Ind.) 2002, 291 F.3d 473, rehearing and rehearing en banc denied.

Habeas petitioner, in order to obtain relief based on a claim of ineffective assistance of counsel, must demonstrate both an identifiable lapse in performance of his attorney and an actual adverse impact on fairness of his trial resulting from the lapse. Taylor v. Maggio, C.A.5 (La.) 1984, 727 F.2d 341. See, also, Rubio v. Estelle, C.A. 5 (Tex.) 1982, 689 F.2d 533; Rinehart v. Brewer, C.A. 8 (Iowa) 1977, 561 F.2d 126.

When counsel is found to be ineffective, court will not bind defendant to state procedural waiver of possible constitutional defenses and the issue may be considered in federal habeas corpus proceeding. Birt v. Montgomery, C.A.11 (Ga.) 1984, 725 F.2d 587, rehearing denied 729 F.2d 1468, certiorari denied 105 S.Ct. 232, 469 U.S. 874, 83 L.Ed.2d 161.

Under some circumstances, incompetency of counsel or ineffective assistance of counsel may rise to the level of violation of federal constitutional rights and may be considered on habeas corpus. Henderson v. Cardwell, C.A.6 (Ohio) 1970, 426 F.2d 150, 27 Ohio Misc. 4, 54 O.O.2d 248, 56 O.O.2d 230.

Defendant who had been denied the effective assistance of counsel in his Texas trial for assault with intent to rape was entitled to habeas corpus relief unless the State of Texas elected within reasonable time to be prescribed by the federal district court to again try the defendant upon the indictment returned against him. Brooks v. State of Tex., C.A.5 (Tex.) 1967, 381 F.2d 619.

State prisoner's claims of ineffective representation were recognizable in habeas corpus proceeding. Fortner v. Balkcom, C.A.5 (Ga.) 1967, 380 F.2d 816.

State court's decision that petitioner was not entitled to habeas corpus relief based on alleged ineffective assistance of counsel was neither "contrary to" nor "an unreasonable application of clearly established Federal law," for purposes of federal habeas corpus statute, as amended by Antiterrorism and Effective Death Penalty Act of 1996 (AEDPA); state court used proper federal standards and reasonably applied standard to facts before it. Archie v. Hobbs, W.D.Va.1997, 954 F.Supp. 1149, appeal dismissed 122 F.3d 1060.

FORM #1

NAME: ___________________

____
ADDRESS:

____

____

____
____
Appearing Pro Se

IN THE UNITED STATES DISTRICT COURT

FOR THE _______________ DISTRICT OF ________________

____

Petitioner,

v.

____

Respondent.

____

REQUEST FOR APPOINTMENT OF COUNSEL IN A FEDERAL HABEAS CORPUS CASE

I.

Introduction

Petitioner ____ hereby respectfully requests that the Court appoint counsel to represent him/her in this matter.

Habeas corpus proceedings "are of fundamental importance . . . in our constitutional scheme because they directly protect our most valued rights." *Brown v. Vasquez*, 952 F.2d 1164, 1169 (9th Cir. 1991) (*quoting Bounds v. Smith*, 430 U.S. 817, 827 (1977)) (citations and internal quotations omitted). Consequently, pursuant to 18 U.S.C. § 3006A(a)(2)(B), this Court has the authority to appoint counsel to

assist an indigent Petitioner if the interests of justice so require. In the present case, Petitioner does not have the financial resources to retain counsel. See Application to Proceed Without Prepayment of Fees and Affidavit (In Forma Pauperis). Rule 8(c) of the Habeas Rules makes clear that district judges have the discretion to order "the appointment of counsel under [the Criminal Justice Act] at any stage of the proceeding."

In deciding whether to appoint counsel, this Court must "evaluate [1] the likelihood of success on the merits as well as [2] the ability of the petitioner to articulate his claims pro se in light of the complexity of the legal issues involved." *Weygandt v. Look*, 718 F.2d 952, 954 (9th Cir. 1983); *accord Rand v. Rowland*, 113 F.3d 1520, 1525 (9th Cir. 1997). As discussed at length in one treatise,

the courts generally have endorsed the appointment of counsel to represent indigent and legally unsophisticated prisoners in the following types of non-capital cases:

> (1) Cases that turn on substantial and complex procedural, legal or mixed legal and factual questions (e.g., the fair composition of grand and petit juries, the voluntariness of confessions, and the effective assistance of counsel).
>
> (2) Cases involving uneducated or mentally or physically impaired petitioners.
>
> (3) Cases likely to require the assistance of experts either in framing or in trying the claims.
>
> (4) Cases in which "'the indigent is in no position to investigate crucial facts.'"
>
> (5) Factually complex cases, e.g., ones involving "conflicting testimony," in which the truth is more likely to "be exposed where both sides are represented

by those trained in the presentation of evidence."

1 R. Hertz & J. Liebman, *Federal Habeas Corpus Practice and Procedure*, § 12.3 (5th ed. 2005) (internal quotations and citations omitted, numbering altered).

In addition, appointment of counsel is mandatory for indigent noncapital petitioners (a) when counsel is "'necessary for effective [use of the] discovery'" procedures[1] and (b) pursuant to Habeas Rule 8(c), if the district court determines that "an evidentiary hearing is warranted."[2]

As set forth below, appointment of counsel is appropriate in this case.

---

[1] Rule 6(a) of the Rules Governing Section 2254 Cases in the United States District Courts.

II. Argument

A. Appointment of counsel is appropriate because this case involves substantial and complex procedural, legal or mixed legal and factual questions.

[2] Rule 8(c) of the Rules Governing Section 2254 Cases in the United States District Courts.

B. Appointment of counsel is appropriate because petitioner lacks education or is mentally or physically impaired.

C. Appointment of counsel is appropriate because this case will probably require the assistance of experts either in framing or in proving the claims.

D. Appointment of counsel is appropriate because the petitioner is indigent and is in no position to investigate crucial facts.

E. Appointment of counsel is appropriate because this is a case in which the parties dispute the facts, and thus the truth is more likely to "be exposed where both sides are represented by those trained in the presentation of evidence."

III. Conclusion

This Court has the authority and should appoint counsel for Petitioner pursuant to 18 U.S.C. §3006A (a)(2)(B). Appointment of counsel will serve the interests of justice and judicial expedience and economy.

Respectfully submitted,

Dated:____________________

____ [signature]

____ [type or print name]

FORM #2

THE HOPKINS LAW OFFICE, P.C.
10645 N. ORACLE RD., #121-326
TUCSON, ARIZONA 85737
TELEPHONE: 520.465.2658
FACSIMILE: 520.867.6509
OBJECTIONYOURHONOR@HOTMAIL.COM

CEDRIC MARTIN HOPKINS, ESQ.
CALIFORNIA STATE BAR NO. 226313
ARIZONA STATE BAR NO. 22790

ATTORNEY FOR ROBERT STANFORD, III

UNITED STATES DISTRICT COURT

DISTRICT OF ARIZONA

Robert Stanford, III, Petitioner, v. Charles L. Ryan, Respondent, Tom Horne, Additional Respondent.	CV 14—00175—PHX—JAT (BSB) PETITION UNDER 28 U.S.C. § 2254 FOR A WRIT OF HABEAS CORPUS BY A PERSON IN STATE CUSTODY (Non-Death Penalty) (Evidentiary Hearing Requested)

Petitioner, Robert Stanford, through his attorney, Cedric Martin Hopkins, Esq., avers as follows:

I.

PARTIES

1.1 Robert Stanford, Petitioner herein, is confined at the Arizona State Prison Complex Florence in Florence, Arizona. On August 17, 2007, a Maricopa County Grand Jury indicted Petitioner on the sole count of second-degree murder. See, Indictment, 08/17/07. A jury found Petitioner guilty of second-degree murder.

1.2 Respondent Charles L. Ryan is the director of the Arizona Department of Corrections where Petitioner is serving his prison term. Tom Horne is the Attorney General for the State of Arizona.

II.

JURISDICTION

2.1 The United States District Court has jurisdiction over the petition for a writ of habeas corpus pursuant to 28 U.S.C. § 2254 and 1331. Petitioner is in custody pursuant to a judgment of an Arizona state court and seeks relief on the ground that his imprisonment and sentence are in violation of his rights under the United States Constitution.

III.

VENUE

3.1 Venue is proper in the United States District Court for the District of Arizona – Phoenix Division because Petitioner's conviction was obtained in the Maricopa County Superior Court, located at 201 W. Jefferson, Phoenix, Arizona 85003. See, 28 U.S.C. § 2241(d).

IV.

PROCEDURAL HISTORY

4.1 On August 17, 2007, a Maricopa County Grand Jury indicted Petitioner on the sole count of second-degree murder.

4.2 On December 9, 2008, the jury returned a guilty verdict for the sole count of second-degree murder against Petitioner.

4.3 On February 20, 2009, Petitioner was sentenced to eighteen years of imprisonment.

V.

APPEALS

5.1 Petitioner filed an appeal to the Court of Appeals, which affirmed his conviction and sentence in a memorandum decision dated May 25, 2010. A petition for review was not filed with the Arizona Supreme Court.

VI.

STATE POST-CONVICTION PROCEEDINGS

6.1 On May 6, 2011, Petitioner filed a petition for post-conviction relief in the Maricopa County Superior Court challenging his sentence and conviction. On September 6, 2011, the Honorable Daniel G. Martin denied Petitioner's petition for post-conviction relief without an evidentiary hearing. See, Maricopa County Superior Court Cause No. CR2007-151813-001 SE.

6.2 On October 4, 2011, Petitioner filed a petition for review with the Arizona Court of Appeals seeking review of the Honorable Daniel G. Martin's decision denying him relief. On August 17, 2012, the Arizona Court of Appeals granted review but denied Petitioner relief and affirmed his sentence and conviction in an unpublished decision. See, Arizona Court of Appeals No. 2 CA-CR 12-0250 PRPC.

6.3 Petitioner filed a discretionary petition for review with the Arizona Supreme Court on September 17, 2012, which was denied on February 15, 2013. See, Arizona Supreme Court Case No. CR-12-0385-PR.

VII.

FEDERAL PROCEEDINGS

7.1 This is the first Federal Petition for Writ of Habeas Corpus filed challenging this conviction.

VIII.

PENDING PROCEEDINGS

8.1 There are no proceedings pending in State court.

IX.

REPRESENTATIONS

9.1 During the pre-trial and trial phases of this case, Petitioner was represented by Lloyd Tate. Lloyd Tate was appointed by the court.

X.

OTHER SENTENCES

10.1 Petitioner is not serving any other prison sentences outside of the prison sentence in CR2007-151813-001 SE.

XI.
GROUNDS FOR RELIEF

11.1 The grounds on which Petitioner contends his conviction are contrary to the Constitution of the United States are fully discussed in the attached Memorandum of Points and Authorities, which is incorporated herein.

11.2 In sum, Petitioner's Due Process rights were violated when his trial counsel provided ineffective assistance of counsel with respect to failing to find, interview, and call as a witness at trial the only eye-witness to the shooting whose testimony would have supported and bolstered Petitioner's claim of self-defense. U.S. Const. Amends. 5, 6, and 14; *Strickland v. Washington*, 466 U.S. 668 (1984).

11.3 After defense counsel's ineffective representation at trial, and after the jury asked to hear from the eye-witness defense counsel failed to call as a witness, the jury found Petitioner guilty of second-degree murder.

11.4 The trial court sentenced Petitioner to eighteen years in prison.

11.5 The trial court denied Petitioner an evidentiary hearing on Petitioner's Petition for Post-Conviction Relief. The trial court, the Arizona Court of Appeals and the Arizona Supreme Court did not grant Petitioner any relief despite the deficient performance of trial counsel and the prejudice suffered by Petitioner as a result thereof.

XII.
EXHAUSTION

12.1 All grounds for relief raised in this petition for writ of habeas corpus have previously been presented to the Arizona Court of Appeals.

12.2 Petitioner has not previously filed any type of petition, application or motion in a federal court regarding the conviction that Petitioner is challenging in this petition.

XIII.
TIMELINESS

13.1 Petitioner's petition is not barred by 28 U.S.C. § 2244(d) because Petitioner has been engaged in the appellate process in the Arizona State Courts since his conviction and therefore the time is tolled pursuant to 28 U.S.C. § 2244(d)(2).

13.2 The Arizona Supreme Court denied Petitioner's Petition for Review on February 15, 2013. Therefore, Petitioner's Petition for Writ of Habeas Corpus was due no later than May 15, 2014, which has already been filed with this Court.

XIV.
RELIEF REQUESTED

WHEREFORE, Petitioner, Robert Stanford, prays that this Court:

14.1 Issue a writ of habeas corpus to have Petitioner brought before the Court to the end that he may be discharged from his unconstitutional conviction;

14.2 Require Respondent to bring forward the entire record of the state court proceedings, and to specify any proceeding in the case that has been reported but not transcribed;

14.3 Require Respondent to file an answer admitting or denying each and every factual allegation herein;

14.4 Allow Petitioner to conduct discovery and to expand the record relating to the issues raised by this petition;

14.5 Conduct an evidentiary hearing at which time proof may be offered concerning the allegations in this petition that Respondent does not admit;

14.6 Issues an order finding that the presumption of correctness does not apply to the questions of law and the mixed questions of law and fact;

14.7 Allow Petitioner sufficient time to brief any other issues of law raised by this petition or this Court; and

14.8 Grant such other and further relief as may be deemed appropriate.

DATED this 11th day of April, 2014.

/s/ Cedric Martin Hopkins

Cedric Martin Hopkins

THE HOPKINS LAW OFFICE, P.C.

VERIFICATION

Cedric Martin Hopkins, attorney for Petitioner in the above-captioned action declares under penalty of perjury that, 1) I have been authorized to file this Petition under 28 U.S.C. § 2254; 2) that I have read the foregoing Petition, and know the contents thereof and the same are true to the best of my knowledge, both in substance and in fact, except as to those matters therein alleged on information and belief which matters I believe to be true.

DATED this 11th day of April, 2014.

/s/ Cedric Martin Hopkins

Cedric Martin Hopkins

THE HOPKINS LAW OFFICE, P.C.

TABLE OF CONTENTS

MEMORANDUM OF POINTS AND AUTHORITIES IN SUPPORT OF THE PETITION FOR A WRIT OF HABEAS CORPUS

I. PROCEDURAL HISTORY AND STATEMENT OF RELEVANT FACTS

The State charged Petitioner with a sole count of second-degree murder for the death of Van Jordan. Petitioner exercised his right to a jury trial with respect to the charge of second-degree murder.

Petitioner admitted to shooting Van Jordan on August 6, 2007. Reporter's Transcript (R.T.), 12/04/08, p. 73:6-8. On that night, Petitioner and Sheikh Ajamu frequented the Redfish Bar in Phoenix, Arizona. Id. at p. 73:9-11. Also on that night, Petitioner carried a gun inside his vehicle for protection. Id. at p. 73:12-16.

While at the Redfish Bar, Petitioner got into a fight and was asked to leave the bar.[1] Id. at p. 74:4 – p. 75:6. Petitioner got into his vehicle, left the parking lot and went to McDonald's. Id. at p. 75:7-16. Petitioner came back to the Redfish Bar to look for girls. Id. at p. 76:1; Id. at p. 90:3-8. While driving in the parking lot, Petitioner stopped his vehicle so that Jordan could pass him. Id. at p. 76:1-6. Petitioner parked, and then Jordan jumped onto the hood of the vehicle. Id. At that point, Petitioner showed Jordan that he had a firearm inside the vehicle. Id. Despite this deterrent, Jordan leaned into the driver's side window, struck Petitioner in the head, and attempted to take the firearm from Petitioner. Id. at p. 77:11-22; Id. at p. 93:18-21. After Jordan reached for the firearm, Petitioner grabbed the gun back and the two yanked it back and forth, engaging in a struggle for the firearm. Id. at p. 78:9-11; Id. at p. 93:10-11. During the struggle for the firearm, Petitioner fired three shots. Id. at p. 78:12-13. Petitioner fired the shots out of fear that Jordan would retrieve the firearm and would then shoot Petitioner. Id. at p. 80:25 – p. 81:3.

Doctor Robert Lyon of the Maricopa County Office of the Medical Examiner performed Jordan's autopsy. R.T., 12/04/08, p. 11:24 – p. 13:21. Dr. Lyon determined that both of Jordan's lungs were penetrated by a single bullet that "exited over the right side of his back." Id. at p. 22:11-14. As a result, Jordan bled to death. Id. at p. 22:15-16. Dr. Lyon stated that he was unable to determine how far away the gun was from Jordan at the time it was fired. Id. at p. 22:22-24. He stated, "there's no evidence of a range of fire." Id. at p. 23:5. Dr. Lyon concluded that the matter of death was homicide. Id. at p. 26:4-5.

---

[1] The fight did not involve the victim, Van Jordan. R.T., 12/04/08, p. 74:19-20.

After considering the evidence and testimony, the jury returned a guilty verdict. R.T., 12/09/08, p. 3:10-15. This Court sentenced Petitioner to an aggravated term of imprisonment of eighteen years. R.T., 02/20/09, p. 30:17-22.

II. JURISDICTIONAL REQUIREMENTS

Petitioner is presently incarcerated in the Arizona State Department of Corrections serving a sentence of 18 years. A state prisoner "whose claim was adjudicated on the merits in state court is not entitled to relief in federal court unless he meets the requirements set forth in 28 U.S.C. § 2254(d)." *Price v. Vincent*, 123 S.Ct. 1848, 1852 (2003). A state prisoner is entitled to federal relief when "he can demonstrate that the state court's adjudication of his claim:" (1) resulted in a decision that was contrary to, or involved an unreasonable application of clearly established federal law, as determined by the Supreme Court of the United States; or (2) resulted in a decision that was based on an unreasonable determination of the facts of the evidence presented in the state court proceeding. Id. quoting, 28 U.S.C. § 2254(d)(1), 1994 ed. Supp. II.).

A state court's decision "is contrary to...clearly established federal law...if the state court applies a rule that contradicts the governing law set forth" in a controlling Supreme Court case, or "if the state court confronts facts that are materially indistinguishable from a relevant Supreme Court precedent and arrives at a result opposite" to the holding. *Williams v. Taylor*, 529 U.S. 362, 405, 412-413 (2000)(Justice O'Connor).

As for "unreasonable application," a federal court may grant relief "if the state court identifies the correct governing legal principle from [the Supreme Court's] decisions but unreasonably applies that principle to the facts of the petitioner's case." Id.;

Ramdass v. Angelone, 530 U.S. 156 (2000); *Busch v. Woodford*, No. 06-16154 (9th Cir., filed 08/29/07). When a claim falls under the "unreasonable application" clause, the state court's application of the Supreme Court precedent must be "objectively unreasonable," not just incorrect. *Wiggins v. Smith*, 539 U.S. 510, 520-521 (2003). Under *Williams v. Taylor*, *supra*, the emphasis of the federal court inquiry is on the nature and quality of the state court decision. *Williams*, 529 U.S. at 420.

In this case, the claim of ineffective assistance of counsel was decided on its merits and not on procedural grounds. The trial court issued an opinion identifying and articulating the legal principles under the federal case, *Strickland v. Washington*, 466 U.S. 668 (1984), which governs these claims and explained the reasons for the denial of the claim. Petitioner contends, however, that the PCR court misunderstood the governing legal principles and incorrectly and unreasonably determined that the governing precedent did not apply or that the PCR court unreasonably applied the law.

Petitioner is raising fundamental federal constitutional and statutory claims. Petitioner contends his constitutional rights have been violated. These violations have resulted in his unconstitutional incarceration and a miscarriage of justice.

III. EXHAUSTION

Before a federal court may review a petitioner's claims on the merits, a petitioner must present in state court every claim raised in the federal habeas petition. This is referred to as the "exhaustion requirement." *Coleman v. Thompson*, 501 U.S. 722, 731 (1991); *Rose v. Lundy*, 455 U.S. 509, 520 (1982). To properly exhaust state remedies, a petitioner must "fairly present" his claims to the state's highest court in a procedurally appropriate manner. *Castille v. Peoples*, 489 U.S. 346, 351 (1989). A non-capital Arizona prisoner must "fairly present" his federal claim to the Arizona Court of Appeals in a procedurally appropriate manner to properly exhaust his state remedies. *Swoopes v. Sublett*, 196 F.3d 1008, 1010 (9th Cir., 1999). In other words, the petitioner must alert the state courts to the federal nature of the claim. *Baldwin v. Reese*, 541 U.S. 27, 32 (2004). If a petitioner failed to fairly present his or her claim to the state courts in a procedurally appropriate manner, the claim is "procedurally defaulted" and barred from federal habeas review. *See, e.g., Ylst v. Nunnemaker*, 501 U.S. 797, 802-805 (1991); *White v. Lewis*, 874 F.2d 599, 602-603 (9th Cir., 1989).

There are two categories of procedural default. The first type of procedural default is when a state court expressly applied a procedural bar to the petitioner's claim when the petitioner raised the claim in state court. *See, e.g., Nunnemaker*, 501 U.S. at 802-805; *Martinez-Villareal v. Lewis*, 80 F.3d 1301, 1305-1306 (9th Cir., 1996). The second type of procedural default occurs when the petitioner failed to even present his claim in state court and returning to state court to present the claim would be futile under the state court's procedural rules. *Teague v. Lane*, 489 U.S. 288, 297-299 (1989); *Reed v. Ross*, 468 U.S. 1, 10-11 (1984).

In this case, Petitioner properly exhausted his claim of ineffective assistance of counsel by raising the issue before the Maricopa County Superior Court, the Arizona Court of Appeals, and the Arizona Supreme Court. Petitioner claimed throughout his state court proceedings that his Due Process rights were violated and his right to effective assistance of counsel under *Strickland v. Washington* was violated. He relied upon and referred the Arizona court to *Strickland v. Washington* regarding his ineffective assistance of counsel claim. As such, Petitioner's claim in this Petition for Writ of Habeas Corpus was properly exhausted.

IV. CLAIMS FOR RELIEF

A. Trial counsel provided ineffective assistance of counsel by failing to find, interview, and call as a witness at trial the only eye-witness to the shooting which the State of Arizona charged Petitioner with second-degree murder when that eye-witness's testimony would have supported Petitioner's claim of self-defense.

To prove ineffective assistance of counsel, a petitioner must show that counsel's representation fell below the standard of care in the profession and that the petitioner was prejudiced. *Strickland v. Washington*, 466 U.S. 668 (1984)(both prongs of test must be satisfied); U.S. Const. Amends. 5, 6 & 14. Whether or not to call a witness to testify can support a claim of ineffective assistance of counsel claim. *Morris v. State of Cal.*, 966 F.2d 448 (Cal. 1991).

Under AEDPA, Petitioner must show not only that a Strickland violation occurred, but also that the state courts' resolution of the claim was not only wrong, but also objectively unreasonable in light of Supreme Court precedent. *Yarborough v. Gentry*, 540 U.S. 1, 6 (2003)(*per curiam*); *Woodford*, 537 U.S. at 25. State courts' rulings on IAC claims are generally analyzed under the unreasonable application prong of § 2254(d)(1); *Weighall v. Middle*, 215 F.3d 1058, 1062 (9th Cir., 2000).

Petitioner's claim of ineffective assistance of counsel centers around one individual: Shiekh Ajamu. Other than the victim and Petitioner, Mr. Ajamu was the only eye-witness to the shooting that led to the victim's death.

During opening statements to the jury, the prosecutor stated, "How about their eye witness version? And that's a little misleading because there are no eyewitnesses. As you'll hear through the police, there's no one who saw this shooting happen except for the victim, who's dead, and the defendant, who did the shooting. There are people who heard it, bouncers at the club, other patrons, but no one saw the shooting." R.T., 12/02/08, p. 7:20-25. Those statements by the prosecutor were not only misleading, but were plainly false.

Reginald Fields, a bouncer at the Redfish Bar, testified that he observed two individuals in the vehicle that was being driven by Petitioner. R.T., 12/03/08, p. 10:10-13. The passenger in the vehicle was Sheikh Ajamu. Attachment A. In fact, Fields stated that he checked both Petitioner, and Ajamu's identification, as well as patted them down for weapons at the time they entered the Redfish Bar. Id. at p. 13:1-6. Without question, Ajamu was in the vehicle at the time of the shooting and observed the entire incident.

Petitioner testified that he shot Jordan in self-defense. R.T., 12/04/08, p. 76:1 – p. 78:13. Ajamu's recollection of the incident is identical to the testimony given by Petitioner at trial. Ajamu recalls Jordan jumping onto the vehicle in an aggressive manner. Attachment A. Ajamu also remembers Jordan leaning into the vehicle fighting with Petitioner. Id. Remarkably, Ajamu attempted to defend Petitioner from Jordan by punching Jordan in the head. Id. Similar to Petitioner's testimony, Ajamu's potential testimony would have been that Petitioner and Jordan were tugging back and forth on the firearm, and that during the struggle the firearm discharged several times. Id. In short, Ajamu's testimony would have been that Jordan attacked Petitioner first, and then, during the struggle, the firearm discharged. Id.

Deficient Performance

Defense counsel chose not to call Ajamu to testify at Petitioner's trial. Defense counsel made this determination because he felt that Ajamu's testimony would be detrimental to Petitioner's case. Attachment B. While defense counsel never interviewed Ajamu (Attachment A), he determined that Ajamu's version of the shooting did not match Petitioner's version. Attachment B. Based on Ajamu's affidavit, however, Ajamu's testimony at trial would have matched Petitioner's testimony and, therefore, bolstered Petitioner's credibility, which played a significant role in this case.

In this case, the State played Petitioner's pre-trial statements that were recorded. R.T., 12/03/08, p. 59:7-12. Those statements gave different accounts as to what occurred the night of the shooting. At trial, Petitioner admitted to giving false statements to the police. R.T., 12/04/08, p. 98:15-17. In other words, the State focused on destroying Petitioner's credibility with the jury. Therefore, it was imperative upon defense counsel to restore Petitioner's credibility. To have Ajamu – the only other eyewitness to the shooting – testify that the incident took place in the same manner as Petitioner described on the witness stand was of utmost importance. Defense counsel's performance was deficient in failing to call Ajamu as a witness.

As stated in Ajamu's affidavit, defense counsel did not interview Ajamu. Attachment A. Defense counsel's position is that he had conversations with Ajamu that led him to believe that Ajamu's recollection of the shooting was different than Petitioner's version. Attachment B. At a minimum, defense counsel should have conducted a thorough interview of Ajamu. Had he done so, then he would have discovered that Ajamu's recollection of the shooting actually matched Petitioner's version of the shooting that he testified to at trial. Attachment A. Both Petitioner and Ajamu recalled the following facts:

1. Neither of them knew Van Jordan.
2. They both walked to Petitioner's vehicle and got inside.
3. Afterwards, Jordan jumped onto the vehicle in an aggressive manner.
4. Jordan also leaned into the vehicle, starting fighting with Petitioner, and attempted to retrieve the firearm that was located inside the vehicle.
5. Petitioner and Jordan began tugging back and forth on the firearm, and during the struggle, several shots were fired.

The testimony enumerated above should have been presented to the jury. Ajamu's testimony would have assisted the jury in deciding Petitioner's guilt or innocence. The jury made this fact clear when it asked: "Why has the defense not called [Ajamu] as a witness?" ROA 73. This layperson, untrained in the law and what amounts to deficient performance in an attorney, understood the importance of having Ajamu testify. The question posed – "Why has the defense not called [Ajamu] as a witness?" was not answered by the Court. Id. Therefore, the jury was at liberty to presume that Ajamu was not called as a witness by the defense because his testimony would have been damaging to Petitioner's case. In other words, the jury must have presumed that what Petitioner had testified to was not what Ajamu would have testified to if called as a witness. Based on Ajamu's affidavit, we know this to be untrue. Ajamu's testimony would have been harmonious with Petitioner's testimony.

Defense counsel failed to ascertain whether Ajamu's testimony coincided with Petitioner's trial testimony. Attachemnt A. Ajamu attempted to speak with defense counsel on several occasions, but defense counsel did not take Ajamu's statement. Id. As a result of not interviewing Ajamu or calling him to testify to the facts noted above, defense counsel's performance was deficient as outlined in *Strickland.*

Prejudice to Petitioner

In spite of defense counsel failing to call Ajamu as a witness at trial, Ajamu became a pivotal person at trial. The jury was focused on Ajamu and Ajamu's potential testimony. On December 3, 2008, the jury asked twice about locating Ajamu. ROA 60, 63; Attachment H. The first question was, "Did Chandler PD try to contact Ashiki [sic] Ajamu from Robert Stanford's phone records?" ROA 60; Attachment H. On the same date a similar jury question was presented: "Did Chandler PD look for Ashiki [sic] Ajamu using Def's. phone records." ROA 63; Attachment H. Neither of these questions were answered for the jury. Id. Their curiosity went unfulfilled.

The following day, the jury asked outright: "Where is Cheek/Sheik?" ROA 73; Attachment H. In demanding an explanation, the jury asked, "Why have we <u>not</u> heard testimony from him?" Id. More directly, the jury posed the question: "Why has the defense <u>not</u> called him as a witness." Id. These questions went unanswered, as well. Id.

Based on the jury's inquiries, it cannot be questioned that the jury valued Ajamu's testimony and that they considered Ajamu's testimony to be crucial. Had the jury been able to hear Ajamu's testimony outlined above – that Jordan was the first aggressor by jumping onto the vehicle, fighting with Petitioner, and struggling for the firearm – then the jury probably would have acquitted Petitioner. The jury would have also heard that

Ajamu actually attempted to defend Petitioner by punching Jordan in the head when Jordan was leaning inside the vehicle. Attachment A. The jury would have had an entirely different view of this case – a view that would have supported Petitioner's innocence and justification for shooting Jordan. Had Ajamu's testimony been presented to the jury, the jury would not have had to ask the telling questions about Ajamu's absence, and would have received Ajamu's testimony that supported Petitioner's testimony. It follows that Petitioner would have been found not guilty of second-degree murder.

Even if a state court previously rejected an ineffective assistance of counsel claim, this Court may still grant habeas relief if the state court's decision was "contrary to, or involved an unreasonable application of, clearly established Federal law, as determined by the Supreme Court of the United States." 28 U.S.C. § 2254(d)(1). Petitioner must show that the state court's decision was "not only erroneous, but objectively unreasonable." *Yarborough*, 540 U.S. at 5.

The Arizona Court of Appeals found that defense counsel's failure to call Mr. Ajamu as a witness at trial was sound trial strategy. This finding was made despite the state courts failing to hold an evidentiary hearing in which defense counsel could have testified at regarding exactly what his trial strategy was in not calling Mr. Ajamu to testify. Petitioner contends that there can be no theory of trial strategy—and none has been presented either by the state, the courts or defense counsel—that can support failing to call the only eyewitness to the shooting, who would have supported a claim of self-defense.

The state court's unsupported and conclusory finding that defense counsel failing to call Mr. Ajamu was sound trial strategy is objectively unreasonable. The decision is objectively unreasonable because of several reasons. First and foremost, Mr. Ajamu's testimony would have supported Petitioner's testimony as to how the victim was the initial aggressor and was attacking Petitioner. Secondly, Doctor Robert Lyon of the Maricopa County Office of the Medical Examiner was unable to determine how far away the gun was from the victim at the time it was fired. R.T., 12/04/08, pp. 22-23. Thirdly, on several occasions, the jury not only requested, but demanded to know where Mr. Ajamu was and why, specifically, defense counsel failed to call him as a witness. The jury questions eradicate any doubt as to Mr. Ajamu's significance in their determination of guilt in this case. If Mr. Ajamu's testimony had been damaging to Petitioner's case or credibility, then it would be sound trial strategy not to call him as a witness. Conversely, if Mr. Ajamu's testimony would support Petitioner's claim of self-defense and would add credibility to Petitioner, then the failure to call him as a witness cannot be said to be sound trial strategy. To find as such is objectively unreasonable.

V. THE PRESUMPTION OF CORRECTNESS PURSUANT TO 28 U.S.C. § 2254(E)(1) DOES NOT APPLY TO THIS CASE WITH RESPECT TO THE MIXED QUESTION OF LAW AND FACT.

Section 2254(d)(2) and (e)(1) provides that a factual determination of a federal issue made by a state court shall be presumed to be correct. That presumption does not apply, however, where the state court proceedings or findings are deficient. Id.; *Townsend v. Sain*, 372 U.S. 293, 318 (1963). A petitioner can rebut the presumption with clear and convincing evidence.

Petitioner contends that the presumption of correctness should not apply to the state's determination that defense counsel provided effective assistance of counsel. The state court's determination that defense counsel provided effective assistance of counsel is a question of law, or at a minimum, a mixed question of law and fact and, as such, the presumption of correctness should not apply.

VI. THIS COURT SHOULD ORDER THAT AN EVIDENTIARY HEARING BE HELD IN ORDER TO DECIDE THE ISSUES PRESENTED.

Petitioner is requesting an evidentiary hearing on the unique and compelling issue presented in this petition. "A petitioner seeking a writ of habeas corpus is entitled to an evidentiary hearing on a claim when (1) the petitioner's allegations, if proved would entitle him to relief, and (2) the state court trier of fact has not, after a full and fair hearing, reliably found the relevant facts." *Williams v. Calderon*, 52 F.3d 1465, 1484 (9th Cir., 1995). Only if the PCR courts have reliably determined the facts of this case may this Court deny a request for an evidentiary hearing. *Tinsley v. Borg*, 895 F.2d 520, 530 (9th Cir., 1990).

In this case, the state and Petitioner dispute the facts as they relate to defense counsel providing ineffective assistance of counsel, and as such, an evidentiary hearing should be granted. *Harris v. Pulley*, 885 F.2d 1354, 1378 (9th Cir., 1988). The PCR court did not conduct an evidentiary hearing and therefore the record is void of any proper evaluation of Petitioner's claim to which this Court can rely. *Totten v. Merkle*, 137 F.3d 1172, 1176 (9th Cir., 1998). As such, Petitioner is entitled to an evidentiary hearing regarding his allegations.

VII. THIS COURT SHOULD REQUIRE THE ARIZONA COURTS OR THE STATE TO TRANSFER THEIR FILES.

In regard to the record, the "[p]etitioner is not required by statute or Rules to attach to his petition or to file a state court record in order to avoid a dismissal for facial insufficiency, although often in summarizing the facts, a petitioner necessarily or as a matter of convenience may refer to state court proceedings and even attach extracts there from." *Bundy v. Wainwright*, 808 F.2d 1410, 1414 (11th Cir., 1987); See, Advisory Committee Note to Rule 5 of the Rules Governing Section 2254 Cases in the United

States District Courts("The obligation to come forward with the state court record is squarely upon the respondent, not upon the petitioner. This makes common sense as well as legal sense—in some cases the petitioner has no copy of the state court proceedings, while the [Habeas] Rules recognize that generally the attorney general has access to them.").

Petitioner requests this Court order the Maricopa County Superior Court, the Arizona Court of Appeals, Division One, or the state prosecutor (County Attorney and/or Attorney General) to forward the complete state court files to this Court in order for this Court to have the entire record available to assure a full and fair review of the issues, both procedurally and substantively. This request is necessary because of the issues involved as well as the procedural history. The entire record is necessary in order to evaluate whether Petitioner was provided due process.

If this Court does not order the state to provide their files in total, it is requested that Petitioner have additional time to amend the record and to submit additional transcripts, pleadings, correspondence, etc., that is in the state record.

VIII. CONCLUSION

Petitioner requests that this Court consider his claim, review the entire record, and base its decision on the totality of the circumstances. Petitioner requests that this Court not presume the state findings are correct with respect to defense counsel providing effective assistance of counsel because of the particulars that are involved in this case.

Then, Petitioner requests this Court conduct an evidentiary hearing and resolve this matter in his favor: vacating his conviction and sentence.

X. RELIEF REQUESTED

Based on the foregoing, Petitioner, Robert Stanford, is entitled to the following relief:

A. An order directing that the state answer this Petition for Writ of Habeas Corpus and order either the state or the state courts to file the entire record from all of the state proceedings with this Court.

B. An order allowing Petitioner to conduct additional necessary discovery.

C. An order finding that this Court has jurisdiction over this matter.

D. An order finding that the presumption of correctness does not apply to whether defense counsel provided effective assistance of counsel.

E. An order finding that the claim raised in this Petition has been exhausted.

F. An order setting an evidentiary hearing so that Petitioner may submit proof of the allegations in this Petition for Writ of Habeas Corpus.

G. Any and all such further relief that this Court deems appropriate.

RESPECTFULLY SUBMITTED this 11th day of April, 2014.

THE HOPKINS LAW OFFICE, P.C.
/s/ Cedric Martin Hopkins
Cedric Martin Hopkins, Esq.

THE HOPKINS LAW OFFICE, P.C.

FORM #3

THE HOPKINS LAW OFFICE, P.C.
10645 N. ORACLE RD., #121-326
TUCSON, ARIZONA 85737
PHONE: 520.465.2658
FAX: 520.867.6509
OBJECTIONYOURHONOR@HOTMAIL.COM

CEDRIC MARTIN HOPKINS
CALIFORNIA BAR NO. 226313
ARIZONA BAR NO. 022790

ATTORNEY FOR PETITIONER

IN THE UNITED STATES DISTRICT COURT

DISTRICT OF ARIZONA

ROBERT B. STANFORD, III, Petitioner, vs. CHARLES RYAN, et. al., Respondents.	CV 14—00175—PHX—JAT **PETITIONER'S OBJECTIONS TO THE REPORT AND RECOMMENDATION**

¶1 Pursuant to Federal Rules of Civil Procedure, Rule 6 and 72 and 28 U.S.C. § 636(b)(1), petitioner makes the following specific objections to the Magistrate's Report and Recommendation:

1. The Magistrate erred in adopting the trial court's finding that "the 'relevant inquiry is not what trial counsel may have chosen to do based on Mr. Ajamu's present testimony, but on what he reasonably believed that testimony would be in 2008 when this matter was being

prepared for trial.'" Report and Recommendation, p. 10, citing Ex. R at 2; Doc. 16-1 at 179). The issue in this case was that trial counsel was not properly prepared for trial in the first place. The basis for that claim is in order for trial counsel to have been properly prepared for trial, it was necessary to conduct a full and thorough interview of the only witness to the shooting. This does not amount to any "distort[ed] effects of hindsight" as found by the Magistrate. Strickland, 466 U.S. at 689.

2. The Magistrate then found that "[i]f the conversation trial counsel had with Ajamu did not indicate that Ajamu's testimony would benefit Petitioner's defense, then it was reasonable for trial counsel to choose not to pursue a formal interview." Report and Recommendation, p. 10. An informal conversation with the only eye-witness to a murder is not sufficient to support a finding that trial counsel did not to explore the witness's potential testimony further. In other words, there is no reasonable explanation for not interviewing Ajamu prior to trial. Investigating Ajamu fully would not have been fruitless, as shown by his affidavit.

3. The Magistrate focuses on trial counsel's self-serving statement that in his informal conversation with Ajamu, Ajamu's statements "did

not match [Petitioner's] story." Report and Recommendation, p. 10, citing Ex. O, Attachment B; Doc. 16-1 at 100-01. The Magistrate's focus is misplaced. Ajamu's clear intent when talking to trial counsel was to ascertain his own potential risk of prosecution. Ajamu was not under oath during these informal conversations and did not provide a full statement, as is obvious from his affidavit.

4. The Magistrate discounts the jury's multiple requests and inquiries regarding why they did not hear from Ajamu, explaining that just because they asked about Ajamu "does not mean that the jury would have believed Ajamu's testimony or given it significant weight." Report and Recommendation, p. 11. The issue is not whether the jury would have believed Ajamu—that would be an impossible standard for Petitioner to meet—the issue is whether Ajamu should have been called as a witness. And the multiple inquiries from the jury refute the Magistrate's suggestion that the jury would not have given Ajamu's testimony significant weight. The jury obviously wanted to hear from him and thought he was a key witness.

5. While the Magistrate found that Petitioner has not shown that a different result would have resulted had Ajamu testified, the jury has already shown it most certainly would have. In other words, had the

jury received what they wanted—Ajamu's testimony—there is a substantial likelihood that the result of the trial would have been different.

¶2 Based on the foregoing, Petitioner respectfully requests that this Court not follow the Magistrate's Report and Recommendation and grant the relief requested.

Dated: April 7, 2015

Respectfully submitted,
THE HOPKINS LAW OFFICE, P.C.

/s/ Cedric Martin Hopkins
Cedric Martin Hopkins
10645 N. Oracle Rd., #121-326
Tucson, Arizona 85737
(520) 465-2658

Attorney for Robert B. Stanford, III

CERTIFICATE OF SERVICE

Undersigned counsel certifies as follows under penalty of perjury:

I hereby certify that Petitioner's Objection to the Report and Recommendation was electronically filed this 7th day of April, 2015, with the Clerk, United States District Court, District of Arizona. I further certify that a copy of the above-captioned Petitioner's Objection to the Report and Recommendation and the transmittal of a Notice of Electronic Filing was delivered electronically and via U.S. Mail on the 7th day of April, 2015, to Arizona Attorney General's Office, 1275 W. Washington, Phoenix, Arizona 85007, attorney for Respondent.

DATED this 7th day of April, 2015.

/s/_______________
Cedric Martin Hopkins, Esq.

FORM # 4

THE HOPKINS LAW OFFICE, P.C.
10645 N. ORACLE RD., #121-326
TUCSON, ARIZONA 85737
PHONE: 520.465.2658
FAX: 520.867.6509
OBJECTIONYOURHONOR@HOTMAIL.COM

CEDRIC MARTIN HOPKINS
CALIFORNIA BAR NO. 226313
ARIZONA BAR NO. 022790

ATTORNEY FOR PETITIONER

IN THE UNITED STATES COURT OF APPEALS

FOR THE NINTH CIRCUIT

ROBERT B. STANFORD, Petitioner, vs. CHARLES RYAN, et. al, Respondents.	No. D.C. Nos. CV-14-00175-PHX-JAT **MOTION FOR CERTIFICATE OF APPEALABILITY**

¶1 Petitioner, Robert B. Stanford, through his attorney, Cedric Martin Hopkins, moves this Court to grant a Certificate of Appealability in accordance with 28 U.S.C. § 2253(c). Stanford wishes to appeal from an Order of a U.S. District Court (Hon. James A. Teilborg) dated July 21, 2015 and filed July 22, 2015, which denied his Petition for Writs of Habeas Corpus (State Custody). (Doc. 21). Stanford also wishes to appeal from the U.S. District Clerk's

Judgment dated and filed July 22, 2015, which dismissed his action and denied Stanford a Certificate of Appealability. (Doc. 22).

Relevant Background

¶2 Stanford's case began in state court (Maricopa County Superior Court) in Maricopa County, Phoenix, Arizona. The State of Arizona charged Stanford with one count of second-degree murder. A jury found Stanford guilty of second-degree murder and Stanford appealed. Following an unsuccessful appeal, Stanford initiated his post-conviction relief proceedings. Without holding a hearing, the trial court denied Stanford's petition for post-conviction relief. Stanford filed a petition for review with the Arizona Court of Appeals, as well as a petition for further review with the Arizona Supreme Court. Both petitions were denied. Stanford's petition for post-conviction relief was premised on his trial counsel failing to call the only eye-witness to the murder. In support of the petition for post-conviction relief, the eyewitness provided an affidavit that would have supported Stanford's position and provided exculpatory evidence.

ISSUE BEFORE THIS COURT

A. WHETHER OR NOT IT IS DEBATABLE THAT TRIAL COUNSEL PROVIDED INEFFECTIVE ASSISTANCE OF COUNSEL BY FAILING TO CALL THE ONLY EYEWITNESS TO THE SHOOTING WHOSE TESTIMONY WOULD HAVE SUPPORTED STANFORD'S SELF-DEFENSE CLAIM.

¶3 There are several striking facets to this case. First, a person lost their life over an exchange outside of a nightclub. Second, that Stanford was convicted of second-degree murder and is serving a lengthy prison sentence. Third, that there was an eyewitness to the shooting. The most striking facet to this case, however, is that the eyewitness was not called to testify at trial. The eyewitness's name is Sheikh Ajamu. Stanford has maintained in the lower courts, including the District Court of Arizona, that his trial counsel was ineffective in failing to call Ajamu to testify at trial.

¶4 In this case, Stanford was asked to leave a bar and crossed paths with the victim, Van Jordan. The two men exchanged heated words and Stanford eventually left the bar parking lot in his vehicle. Jordan was also asked the leave the bar and was escorted to his vehicle. At that same time, Stanford had driven back into the bar parking lot looking to talk to women leaving the bar. Stanford saw Jordan walking in the parking lot and stopped his car so that Jordan could walk by. Stanford then parked his vehicle. At that time, Jordan jumped onto the hood of Stanford's vehicle. At that point, Stanford showed Jordan that he had a firearm inside the vehicle in an effort to get Jordan to back away. Despite this deterrent, Jordan leaned into the driver's side window, struck Stanford in the head with his fist, and attempted to take the firearm from Petitioner. After Jordan reached for the firearm, Stanford grabbed the gun back and the two yanked it back and forth, engaging in a struggle for the firearm. During the struggle for the firearm, Stanford fired three shots. Stanford fired the shots out of fear that Jordan would retrieve the firearm and would then shoot Stanford.

¶5 During all interactions with Jordan, Ajamu was present with Stanford. Reginald Fields, a bouncer at the Redfish Bar, testified that he observed two individuals in the vehicle that was being driven by Stanford. R.T., 12/03/08, p. 10:10-13. That second individual was Ajamu. Ajamu provided an affidavit during the post-conviction relief proceedings that indicated Jordan jumped onto the vehicle in an aggressive manner. Ajamu also remembered Jordan leaning into the vehicle fighting with Stanford. Remarkably, Ajamu attempted to defend Stanford from Jordan by punching Jordan in the head. Similar to Stanford's testimony, Ajamu's testimony would have been that Stanford and Jordan were tugging back and forth on the firearm, and that during the struggle the firearm discharged several times. In short, Ajamu's testimony would have been that Jordan attacked Stanford first, and then, during the struggle, the firearm discharged.

¶6 Not only did Stanford feel Ajamu should have been called to testify, so did the jury. The jury made this fact clear when it asked: "Why has the defense not called [Ajamu] as a witness?" ROA 73. It is certainly debatable whether Ajamu should have been called as a witness and whether the failure to do so prejudiced Stanford. In the first instance, the question indicates the jury wanted to hear from Ajamu. More to the point of prejudice, the question specifically asks why Stanford ("the defense") did not call Ajamu. The question did not ask why the State did not call Ajamu, but rather why Stanford did not call Ajamu. The jury placed a high enough premium on Ajamu's testimony that they listened to the testimony, wrote out the question and submitted it to the judge for an answer. In fact, the jury ask five questions directly asking about Ajamu, his whereabouts and his lack of testimony.

¶7 The first question was, "Did Chandler PD try to contact Ashiki [sic] Ajamu from Robert Stanford's phone records?" ROA 60; Attachment H. On the same date a similar jury question was presented: "Did Chandler PD look for Ashiki [sic] Ajamu using Def's. phone records." ROA 63; Attachment H. Neither of these questions were answered for the jury.

¶8 The following day, the jury asked outright: "Where is Cheek/Sheik?" ROA 73; Attachment H. In demanding an explanation, the jury asked, "Why have we not heard testimony from him?" Id. More directly, the jury posed the question: "Why has the defense not called him as a witness." Id.

¶9 Given what Ajamu would have testified to, coupled with the jury's insistence in wanting to hear from Ajamu, it is debatable whether trial counsel provided ineffective assistance of counsel in failing to call Ajamu as a witness.

¶10 The District Court Judge of Arizona focused on an email sent from Stanford's trial counsel to undersigned counsel that indicated trial counsel did not call Ajamu as a witness because Ajamu "did not give me information that was exculpatory for [Stanford]." Ajamu's affidavit proves otherwise. Trial counsel's email also indicated that Ajamu's version of events did not match Stanford's story, but also indicated that Stanford's story had "changed frequently." Stanford testified at trial. Presumably, trial counsel knew prior to Stanford testifying what version of events Stanford was going to testify to at trial. Ajamu's affidavit and Stanford's trial testimony are harmonious. Trial counsel's after-the-fact email does not insulate him from his failure to interview and call Ajamu as a witness.

¶11 With respect to prejudice, the District Court Judge indicated that it is insufficient to simply make the argument that Ajamu should have been called as a witness, but rather Stanford must show that "there would have been a substantial chance that the outcome would have been different." Doc 21, p. 7, citing *Harrington v. Richter*, 562 U.S. 86, 112 (2011). The District Court Judge did acknowledge, however, that the jury's requests to hear from Ajamu "drew a negative inference from Ajamu's failure to testify." Doc. 21, p. 8. Had trial counsel called Ajamu to testify, then that negative inference would not have been present. And as shown above, the jury explicitly placed great weight on Ajamu's testimony. And had Ajamu testified, there would have been a substantial chance the jury would have believed Stanford—Ajamu's testimony surely would have supported Stanford's testimony. As it was, Stanford's testimony was not only not supported by Ajamu's lack of testimony, the lack of testimony was used against him ("negative inference was draw).

¶12 The District Court Judge then focuses on the "objective" evidence against Stanford and cites a police detective's belief that shell casings should have landed in the vehicle if the shooting happened as Stanford testified. Doc. 21, p. 8. The District Court Judge also referenced Doctor Robert Lyon's (the forensic pathologist) testimony. Dr. Lyon performed Jordan's autopsy and made certain findings. The District Court Judge focused only on the finding that powder burns were not on the victim's hands, which would have been the case if the victim were holding onto the gun when it was discharged. Doc. 21, p. 8. The District Court Judge also focused on the victim's shirt not having gunpowder residue on it. These findings were used to find that "the strength of the government's evidence" would have been controlling for the jury.

¶13 What the District Court Judge failed to reference or discuss was Dr. Lyon finding that he was unable to determine how far away the gun was from Jordan at the time it was fired. Id. at p. 22:22-24. Dr. Lyon's testimony was that "there's no evidence of a range of fire." Id. at p. 23:5. Instead, the District Court Judge focused on what should have been or what the detective believed should have happened instead of Dr. Lyon's empirical finding that, given the evidence, it was impossible to tell how far away the gun was from Jordan when it was fired.

¶14 The issue before this Court then, is whether it is debatable trial counsel provided ineffective assistance of counsel. That is, whether Ajamu should have been interviewed and called as a witness given the statements made by Ajamu in his affidavit.

Standard of Review

¶15 Under *Miller-El v. Cockrell*, 537 U.S. 322 (2003), Stanford need not show that he is probably correct, or even that there is a substantial likelihood that he is correct in order to obtain a certificate of appealability. A certificate of appealability is required if Stanford demonstrates that reasonable jurists would find the district court's assessment of Stanford's claim debatable. Id. at

338. With the instructions provided by the *Miller-El* Court, along with Stanford's arguments outlined above, a certificate of appealability is warranted in this case. In any event, a certificate of appealability should issue given that the issues presented by Stanford are "'adequate to deserve encouragement to proceed further.'" *Slack v. McDaniel*, 529 U.S. 473, 484 (2000)(quoting *Barefoot v. Estelle*, 463 U.S. 880, 893, n.4 (1983)).

CONCLUSION

¶16 Stanford has raised legitimate issues relating to trial counsel providing ineffective assistance of counsel for failing to call the only eyewitness to the shooting, even when the jury was asking why Stanford was not calling that witness and the witness would have corroborated Stanford's testimony. Jurists of reason would find Judge Teilborg's rulings relating to these issues debatable. This Court should issue a Certificate of Appealability so that Judge Teilborg's orders and judgment may be reviewed on appeal.

¶17 Stanford respectfully requests that this motion be assigned to a three-judge panel, and that oral argument be held.

Dated: August 19, 2015

Respectfully submitted,
THE HOPKINS LAW OFFICE, P.C.

/s/____________________

Cedric Martin Hopkins
10645 N. Oracle Rd., #121-326
Tucson, Arizona 85737
(520) 465-2658

CERTIFICATE OF SERVICE

Undersigned counsel certifies as follows under penalty of perjury:

I hereby certify that Petitioner's Motion for Certificate of Appealability was electronically filed this 19th day of August, 2015, with the Clerk, United States District Court. I further certify that a copy of the above-captioned Motion for Certificate of Appealability was delivered electronically and via U.S. Mail on the 19th day of August, 2015, to Arizona Attorney General's Office, Adele Ponce, Esq., 1275 W. Washington, Phoenix, Arizona 85007, attorney for Respondent.

DATED this 19th day of August, 2015.

/s/________________

Cedric Martin Hopkins, Esq.

FORM #5

No. 15-16652

UNITED STATES COURT OF APPEALS
FOR THE NINTH CIRCUIT

ROBERT B. STANFORD, III,
Petitioner-Appellant,

v.

CHARLES RYAN, et. al.,
Respondent-Appellees.

ON APPEAL FROM THE UNITED STATES DISTRICT COURT
FOR THE DISTRICT OF ARIZONA

BRIEF OF APPELLANT ROBERT B. STANFORD, III

CEDRIC MARTIN HOPKINS
THE HOPKINS LAW OFFICE, P.C.
10645 N. Oracle Rd., #121-326
Tucson, Arizona 85737
(520) 465-2658

May 24, 2016

Counsel for Robert B. Stanford, III

TABLE OF CONTENTS

TABLE OF AUTHORITIES

Case Law

U.S. Constitution

Statutes

Rules

I. JURISDICTIONAL STATEMENT

Following the District Court's denial of his Petition for Writ of Habeas Corpus—both the Magistrate Judge's Report and Recommendations (ER 11) and the District Judge's Decision (ER 2)—Appellant, Robert Stanford, III ("Stanford") filed a Notice of Appeal (ER 1) and a Motion for Certificate of Appealability with this Court. On February 16, 2016, Stanford's motion was granted with respect to the issue relating to trial counsel providing ineffective assistance of counsel. Because a Certificate of Appealability has been issued, this Court has jurisdiction to rule on the merits of Stanford's claims. 28 U.S.C. § 2253(c)(1); *Miller-El v. Cockrell*, 537 U.S. 322, 335-336, 123 S.Ct. 1029, 1039, 154 L.Ed.2d 931 (2003).

II. STATEMENT OF ISSUES

1. Whether trial counsel's failure to adequately interview or call as a witness during Stanford's trial the only eye-witness to the shooting supports a finding of ineffective assistance of counsel when that witness's testimony would have buoyed Stanford's self-defense claim and the jury repeatedly asked to hear from the eye-witness.

2. Whether Stanford's claim is procedurally defaulted based on a State bar when he has given the State courts a full and fair opportunity to correctly resolve the case.

III. STATEMENT OF THE CASE

In a single-count indictment, the State of Arizona charged Stanford with second-degree murder for the death of Van Jordan. ER 95. Stanford exercised his right to a jury trial with respect to the charge of second-degree murder. Stanford does not dispute shooting Van Jordan, but has maintained that the shooting was done in self-defense. ER 58.

Stanford exercised his right to a jury trial on the indictment and, after considering the evidence and testimony, the jury returned a guilty verdict. ER 45. The Maricopa County Superior Court sentenced Stanford to an aggravated term of imprisonment of eighteen years. ER 41.

Stanford challenged his conviction under State post-conviction proceedings by filing a petition for post-conviction relief. Stanford argued that his trial counsel, Loyd Tate, provided ineffective assistance of counsel by not properly interviewing and calling Sheikh Ajamu as a witness during trial. Ajamu was the only eyewitness to the shooting and would have provided testimony that supports Stanford's self-defense claim. The trial court denied the petition for post-conviction relief without conducting an evidentiary hearing to consider either Tate or Ajamu's testimony. ER 30. The trial court found that Tate's failure to interview or call Ajamu as a witness did not constitute ineffective assistance of counsel. Id.

Stanford filed a petition for review to the Arizona Court of Appeals and the Arizona Supreme Court. Both petitions were denied. ER 24-25.

Stanford then filed a timely Petition for Writ of Habeas Corpus in Federal Court, District of Arizona. The Honorable Eileen S. Willett, United States Magistrate Judge, filed a Report and Recommendation that recommended dismissal of Stanford's petition. ER 11. District Court Judge, James A. Teilborg denied Stanford's Petition and denied a certificate of appealability. ER 2. Stanford filed a notice of appeal (ER 1) and challenged the District Court's denial of a certificate of appealability with this Court and, on February 16, 2016, Circuit Judges Trott and Watford issued an order granting Stanford's request for a certificate of appealability. This brief follows.

IV. STATEMENT OF RELEVANT FACTS

On August 6, 2007, Stanford and Sheikh Ajamu patronized the Redfish Bar in Phoenix, Arizona. ER 58. While at the Redfish Bar, Stanford got into a fight (the fight did not involve Jordan) and was asked to leave the bar. ER 59-60. Stanford got into his vehicle, left the parking lot and went to McDonald's to eat. ER 60.

Stanford came back to the Redfish Bar to socialize in the parking lot after the bar closed. ER 61, 75. While driving in the parking lot, however, Stanford stopped his vehicle so that Jordan could pass him. ER 61. Stanford parked and then Jordan jumped onto the hood of the vehicle. Id. At that point, Stanford showed Jordan that he had a firearm inside the vehicle. Id. Despite this deterrent, Jordan leaned into the driver's side window, struck Stanford in the head with a closed fist, and attempted to take the firearm from Stanford. ER 62, 78.

After Jordan reached for the firearm, Stanford grabbed the gun back and the two yanked it back and forth, engaging in a struggle for the firearm. ER 63, 78. During the struggle for the firearm, Stanford fired three shots. ER 63. Stanford fired the shots out of fear that Jordan would retrieve the firearm and would then shoot Stanford. ER 65-66.

Doctor Robert Lyon of the Maricopa County Office of the Medical Examiner performed Jordan's autopsy. ER 54. Dr. Lyon determined that both of Jordan's lungs were penetrated by a single bullet that "exited over the right side of his back." ER 55. As a result, Jordan bled to death. Id. **Dr. Lyon stated that he was unable to determine how far away the gun was from Jordan at the time it was fired.** Id. He stated, "there's no evidence of a range of fire." ER 56. Dr. Lyon concluded that the matter of death was homicide. ER 57.

Sheikh Ajamu was a passenger in Stanford's vehicle at the time Jordan jumped onto the vehicle and struck Stanford in the face. ER 35. Ajamu attempted to defend Stanford from Jordan by punching Jordan in the head while Jordan was attacking Stanford. Id. Ajamu witnessed Jordan and Stanford struggling for the firearm and heard the firearm discharge several times. Id. Ajamu attempted to give his full statement to Tate, but Tate did not follow up with Ajamu to interview him or call him as a witness. Id. The jury asked about the whereabout of Ajamu on several occasions. ER 46-50.

V. SUMMARY OF THE ARGUMENT

Once Tate learned that Ajamu could have potential exculpatory or supportive testimony on behalf of Stanford, he was obligated to adequately interview Ajamu in order to obtain his complete statement. Ajamu attempted to provide Tate with his full statement by calling Tate's office and did not receive a return telephone call. Tate never interviewed Ajamu or called him as a witness.

Under *Strickland v. Washington*, 466, U.S. 668 (1984), and *Morris v. State of Cal.*, 966 F.2d 448 (Cal.1991), Tate provided ineffective assistance of counsel by failing to adequately interview Ajamu prior to trial in order to obtain Ajamu's full statement. Tate also provided ineffective assistance of counsel by failing to call Ajamu as a witness to the shooting. The jury's questions as to why Ajamu did not testify demonstrates the prejudice Stanford suffered as a result of Tate failing to present Ajamu's testimony. Finally, Standford's claims are not procedurally defaulted based on an implied state bar because he fairly presented his arguments to the highest State court and gave the State court a full and fair opportunity to resolve the federal issues.

VI. ARGUMENT

A. TRIAL COUNSEL'S FAILURE TO ADEQUATELY INTERVIEW OR CALL AS A WITNESS DURING STANFORD'S TRIAL THE ONLY EYE-WITNESS TO THE SHOOTING SUPPORTS A FINDING OF INEFFECTIVE ASSISTANCE OF COUNSEL WHEN THAT WITNESS'S TESTIMONY WOULD HAVE BUOYED STANFORD'S SELF-DEFENSE CLAIM AND THE JURY REPEATEDLY ASKED TO HEAR FROM THE EYE-WITNESS.

Standard of Review

The Court of Appeals reviews de novo the district court's decision to grant or deny a habeas corpus petition. *Jensen v. Pliler*, 439 F.3d 1086, 1088 (9th Cir. 2006).

Discussion

To prove ineffective assistance of counsel, a petitioner must show that counsel's representation fell below the standard of care in the profession and that the petitioner was prejudiced. *Strickland v. Washington*, 466 U.S. 668 (1984)(both prongs of test must be satisfied); U.S. Const. Amends. 5, 6 & 14. Whether or not to call a witness to testify can support a claim of ineffective assistance of counsel claim. *Morris v. State of Cal.*, 966 F.2d 448 (Cal. 1991).

Under AEDPA, Stanford must show not only that a *Strickland* violation occurred, but also that the state courts' resolution of the claim was not only wrong, but also objectively unreasonable in light of Supreme Court precedent.

Yarborough v. Gentry, 540 U.S. 1, 6 (2003)(*per curiam*). State courts' rulings on IAC claims are generally analyzed under the unreasonable application prong of § 2254(d)(1); *Weighall v. Middle*, 215 F.3d 1058, 1062 (9th Cir., 2000).

Sheikh Ajamu is the foundation of Stanford's issue before this Court. In this case, the prosecutor—during trial—attempted to remove Ajamu from the jury's consideration and Stanford's trial counsel actually excluded Ajamu from trial. Strikingly, other than the victim and Stanford. Ajamu was the only eyewitness to the shooting that led to the victim's death. And the only entity—other than Stanford, himself—who demanded to hear from Ajamu was the jury.

During opening statements to the jury, the prosecutor stated,

> "How about their eye witness version? And that's a little misleading because there are no eyewitnesses. As you'll hear through the police, there's no one who saw this shooting happen except for the victim, who's dead, and the defendant, who did the shooting. There are people who heard it, bouncers at the club, other patrons, but no one saw the shooting." ER 94.

Reginald Fields, a bouncer at the Redfish Bar, testified that he observed two individuals in the vehicle Stanford was driving. ER 90. The passenger in the vehicle was Ajamu. ER 35. In fact, Fields stated that he checked both Stanford and Ajamu's identification, as well as patted them down for weapons at the time they entered the Redfish Bar. ER 91. Without question, Ajamu was in the vehicle at the time of the shooting and observed the entire incident.

Stanford testified that he shot Jordan in self-defense. ER 61-63. Ajamu's recollection of the incident is identical to the testimony given by Stanford at trial. Ajamu recalls Jordan jumping onto the vehicle in an aggressive manner. ER 35. Ajamu also remembers Jordan leaning into the vehicle fighting with Stanford. Id. Remarkably, Ajamu attempted to defend Stanford from Jordan by punching Jordan in the head. Id. Similar to Stanford's testimony, Ajamu's potential testimony would have been that Stanford and Jordan were tugging back and forth on the firearm, and that during the struggle the firearm discharged several times. Id. In short, Ajamu's testimony would have been that Jordan attacked Stanford first, and then, during the struggle, the firearm discharged. Id.

Deficient Performance

Tate chose not to call Ajamu to testify at Stanford's trial. Tate made this determination because he felt that Ajamu's testimony would be detrimental to Stanford's case. ER 39. Tate made that decision based on informal, momentary remarks Ajamu made to Tate at court hearings. ER 35, 39. Tate never actually interviewed Ajamu (ER 35), yet he determined that Ajamu's version of the shooting did not match Stanford's version. ER 39. Based on

Ajamu's affidavit, however, Ajamu's testimony at trial would have matched Stanford's testimony and, therefore, bolstered Stanford's credibility, which played a significant role in this case.

In this case, the State played Stanford's pre-trial statements that were recorded. ER 92. Those statements gave different accounts as to what occurred the night of the shooting. At trial, Stanford admitted to giving false statements to the police. ER 83. In other words, the State focused on destroying Stanford's credibility with the jury. Therefore, it was imperative upon Tate to restore Stanford's credibility. To have Ajamu – the only other eyewitness to the shooting – testify that the incident took place in the same manner as Stanford described on the witness stand was of utmost importance. Tate's performance was deficient in failing to call Ajamu as a witness.

As stated in Ajamu's affidavit, Tate did not interview Ajamu. ER 35. Tate's position is that he had brief exchanges with Ajamu that led him to believe that Ajamu's recollection of the shooting was different than Stanford's version. ER 39. Based on Tate's statements, however, Ajamu was more concerned with asking Tate about his own risk for being in the vehicle, not providing Tate with a complete statement. Id. At a minimum, Tate should have conducted a thorough interview of Ajamu. Had he done so, then he would have discovered that Ajamu's recollection of the shooting actually matched Stanford's version of the shooting that he testified to at trial. ER 35. Both Stanford and Ajamu recalled the following facts:

1. Neither of them knew Van Jordan.
2. They both walked to Stanford's vehicle and got inside.
3. Afterwards, Jordan jumped onto the vehicle in an aggressive manner.
4. Jordan also leaned into the vehicle, starting fighting with Stanford, and attempted to retrieve the firearm that was located inside the vehicle.
5. Stanford and Jordan began tugging back and forth on the firearm, and during the struggle, several shots were fired. ER 35.

The testimony enumerated above should have been presented to the jury.

Jury's Demand to Hear Ajamu's Testimony

Ajamu's testimony would have assisted the jury in deciding Stanford's guilt or innocence. The jury made this fact clear when it asked: "Why has the defense <u>not</u> called [Ajamu] as a witness?" ER 46 (emphasis in original). This layperson, untrained in the law and what amounts to deficient performance in an attorney, understood the importance of having Ajamu testify. The question posed – "Why has the defense <u>not</u> called [Ajamu] as a witness?" was not answered by the Court. Id. Therefore, the jury was at liberty to presume that

Ajamu was not called as a witness by the defense because his testimony would have been damaging to Stanford's case. In other words, the jury must have presumed that what Stanford had testified to was not what Ajamu would have testified to if called as a witness. Based on Ajamu's affidavit, we know this assumption to be untrue, however the assumption went unaddressed. Ajamu's testimony would have been harmonious with Stanford's testimony and would have had the potential to significantly reinforce Stanford's self-defense claim.

Tate failed to ascertain whether Ajamu's testimony coincided with Stanford's trial testimony. ER 35. Ajamu attempted to speak with Tate on several occasions, but Tate did not take Ajamu's statement. Id. As a result of not interviewing Ajamu or calling him to testify to the facts noted above, Tate's performance was deficient as outlined in *Strickland.*

Prejudice to Stanford

In spite of Tate failing to call Ajamu as a witness at trial, Ajamu became a pivotal person at trial. The jury was focused on Ajamu and Ajamu's potential testimony. On December 3, 2008, the jury asked twice about locating Ajamu. ER 48-49. The first question was, "Did Chandler PD try to contact Ashiki [sic] Ajamu from Robert Stanford's phone records?" ER 48. On the same date a similar jury question was presented: "Did Chandler PD look for Ashiki [sic] Ajamu using Def's. phone records." ER 49. Neither of these questions were answered for the jury. Id. Yet again, their curiosity went unfulfilled.

The following day, the jury asked outright: "Where is Cheek/Sheik?" ER 46. In demanding an explanation, the jury asked, "Why have we not heard testimony from him?" Id. (emphasis in original). More directly, the jury posed the question: "Why has the defense not called him as a witness." Id. These questions went unanswered, as well. Id.

Based on the jury's inquiries, it cannot be questioned that the jury valued Ajamu's testimony and that they considered Ajamu's testimony to be crucial. Had the jury been able to hear Ajamu's testimony outlined above – that Jordan was the first aggressor by jumping onto the vehicle, fighting with Stanford, and struggling for the firearm – then the jury probably would have acquitted Stanford. The jury would have also heard that Ajamu actually attempted to defend Stanford by punching Jordan in the head when Jordan was leaning inside the vehicle. ER 35. The jury would have had an entirely different view of this case – a view that would have supported Stanford's innocence and justification for shooting Jordan. Had Ajamu's testimony been presented to the jury, the jury would not have had to ask the telling questions about Ajamu's absence, and would have received Ajamu's testimony that supported

Stanford's testimony. It follows that Stanford would have been found not guilty of second-degree murder.

Even if a state court previously rejected an ineffective assistance of counsel claim, this Court may still grant habeas relief if the state court's decision was "contrary to, or involved an unreasonable application of, clearly established Federal law, as determined by the Supreme Court of the United States." 28 U.S.C. § 2254(d)(1). Stanford must show that the state court's decision was "not only erroneous, but objectively unreasonable." *Yarborough*, 540 U.S. at 5.

The Arizona Court of Appeals found that Tate's failure to call. Ajamu as a witness at trial was sound trial strategy. This finding was made despite the state courts failing to hold an evidentiary hearing in which Tate could have testified at regarding exactly what his trial strategy was in not calling Ajamu to testify. Stanford contends that there can be no theory of trial strategy—and none has been presented either by the state, the courts or Tate—that can support failing to adequately interview or call the only eyewitness to the shooting who would have supported a claim of self-defense.

The state court's unsupported and conclusory finding that Tate failing to call Ajamu was sound trial strategy is objectively unreasonable. The decision is objectively unreasonable because of several reasons. First and foremost,

Ajamu's testimony would have supported Stanford's testimony as to how the victim was the initial aggressor and was attacking Stanford. Secondly, Doctor Robert Lyon of the Maricopa County Office of the Medical Examiner was unable to determine how far away the gun was from the victim at the time it was fired. ER 55-56. Thirdly, on several occasions, the jury not only requested, but demanded to know where Ajamu was and why, specifically, Tate failed to call him as a witness. ER 46-49. The jury's questions eradicate any doubt as to Ajamu's significance in their determination of guilt in this case. If Ajamu's testimony had been damaging to Stanford's case or credibility, then it would be sound trial strategy not to call him as a witness. Conversely, if Ajamu's testimony would support Stanford's claim of self-defense and would add credibility to Stanford, then the failure to call him as a witness cannot be said to be sound trial strategy.

Ajamu's affidavit highlights how his testimony would have supported Stanford's testimony and theory of self-defense. Ajamu's testimony directly contradicted the State's theory of the case—that Stanford shot Jordan intentionally and not in self-defense. Other than Stanford's own testimony, Ajamu's testimony was the only other definitive evidence that Stanford acted in self-defense. Tate's statements disclose an implied admission that he did not adequately interview Ajamu. Tate stated that he told the prosecutor and investigator about Ajamu but no one interviewed Ajamu. A defense attorney cannot simply ignore the most beneficial evidence of a client's self-defense claim and then use the strategy shield to avoid a finding of ineffective assistance of counsel. Tate had an obligation to properly interview Ajamu and ascertain exactly what his testimony would be. Following that interview, Tate could then form a legitimate decision to either call Ajamu as a witness or not, after conferring with Stanford. Tate failed to even take the first step in adequately interviewing Ajamu. A couple of momentary remarks with Ajamu about Ajamu's potential risk do not qualify as to properly interviewing the only eyewitness to a potential murder conviction.

B. STANFORD'S CLAIM IS NOT PROCEDURALLY DEFAULTED BASED ON A STATE LAW BAR BECAUSE HE HAS GIVEN THE STATE COURTS A FULL AND FAIR OPPORTUNITY TO CORRECTLY RESOLVE THE ISSUE.

Standard of Review

The Court of Appeals reviews de novo the district court's decision to grant or deny a habeas corpus petition. *Jensen v. Pliler*, 439 F.3d 1086, 1088 (9th Cir. 2006). The issue of whether a federal claim was properly exhausted in state court is reviewed de novo. *Vang v. Nevada*, 329 F.3d 1069, 1072 (9th Circ. 2003).

The Exhaustion Requirement

The procedural bar doctrine is a subcategory of the independent and adequate state ground doctrine. *Robinson v. Schriro*, 595 F.3d 1086, 1100 (9th Cir. 2010), *citing Boyd v. Thompson*, 147 F.3d 1124, 1126 (9th Circ. 1998). Under the procedural bar doctrine, a federal court ordinarily will not review a state court ruling if the state court would find that the claim was barred pursuant to an independent and adequate state procedural rule. Id. This Court recognizes two types of procedural bars: express and implied. *Robinson*, 595 F.3d at 1100. At issue herein is the implied procedural bar, which occurs when the petitioner has failed to fairly present his claims to the highest state court and would now be barred by a state procedural rule from doing so. Id.

1. Stanford Exhausted His Federal Claims. Therefore, His Claims are not Subject to a Procedural Bar.

Claims of Arizona state prisoners are exhausted for purposes of federal habeas once the Arizona Court of Appeals has ruled on them. *Swoopes v. Sublett*, 196 F.3d 1008, 1010 (9th Cir. 1999).

In order to exhaust his claim, Stanford was required to present both the factual and legal basis for the claim to the state court. *Robinson*, 595 F.3d at 1101. To do so, Stanford was required to reference specific provisions of the federal constitution or cite to federal case law and to provide a statement of the facts that entitle him to relief. *Robinson*, 595 F.3d at 1101. In other words, Stanford needed to present the highest State court with a factual and legal basis for his claims. *Duncan v. Henry*, 513 U.S. 364, 365, 115 S.Ct. 887, 130 L.Ed.2d 865 (1995) (legal basis); *Kenney v. Tamayo-Reyes*, 504 U.S. 1, 112 S.Ct. 1715, 1719, 118 L.Ed.2d 318 (1992) (factual basis).

Stanford presented the factual basis for his claim in his petition for post-conviction relief as well as in his petition for review to the Arizona Court of Appeals and in his discretionary petition for review to the Arizona Supreme Court. Stanford also presented the legal basis for his claim to the state court, citing to federal case law as shown herein below.

Stanford raised a claim of ineffective assistance of counsel since the inception of his post-conviction relief proceedings. In his petition for post-conviction relief, Stanford premised his ineffective assistance of counsel claims on *Strickland v. Washington*, 466, U.S. 668 (1984), as well as the United States Consitution, Amendments 5, 6 and 14. He also argued that failure to call a witness can support his ineffective assistance of counsel claim under *Morris v. State of Cal.*, 966 F.2d 448 (Cal.1991).

Stanford extended his federal claims in his petition for review to the Arizona State Court of Appeals, as well as to the Arizona Supreme Court. In addition, the trial court and Arizona Court of Appeals both decided Stanford's ineffective assistance of counsel claim by analyzing federal law, namely *Strickland*. ER 25-34. The Arizona Supreme Court denied relief without comment. ER 24.

For the reasons set forth above, Stanford fairly presented his claims to the highest state court and he was not barred by any state procedural rules from doing so. Stanford is, therefore, entitled to have his ineffective assistance of counsel claim pursuant to *Strickland* decided on its merits.

VII. CONCLUSION

Tate did not adequately interview Ajamu prior to trial. The jury, through its questions submitted during trial, showed how important of a witness Ajamu was for Stanford's claim of self-defense. Based on Ajamu's affidavit, Ajamu's testimony would have supported Stanford's theory of self-defense. Tate was unaware of Ajamu's impending testimony because he failed to adequately interview him. Tate did not call Ajamu as a witness because he failed to ascertain exactly what Ajamu would have testified to due to not having adequately interviewed Ajamu. Tate's inaction in this case constitutes ineffective assistance of counsel and Stanford was prejudice by that inaction as shown by the jury's demand for Ajamu's testimony.

VIII. CERTIFICATE OF COMPLIANCE

I certify that this brief complies with the type-volume limitation set forth in Rule 32(a)(7)(B) of the Federal Rules of Appellate Procedure. This brief uses a proportional typeface and 14-point font, and contains 3,981 words.

IX. STATEMENT OF RELATED CASES

Stanford is not aware of any cases pending in this Court that would be deemed related pursuant to Ninth Circuit Rule 28-2.6.

DATED: May 24, 2016

Respectfully submitted,

THE HOPKINS LAW OFFICE, P.C.

By: s/ Cedric Martin Hopkins
Cedric Martin Hopkins
Attorney for Stanford-Appellant

PROOF OF SERVICE

Undersigned counsel certifies as follows under penalty of perjury:

I hereby certify that the Brief of Appellant Robert Stanford, III was electronically filed this 24th day of May, 2016, with the Clerk, United States Court of Appeals, Ninth Circuit, 95 Seventh Street, San Francisco, California, 94103. I further certify that a copy of the above-captioned Brief of Appellant Robert Stanford, III, along with a copy of the Excerpt of Record, was delivered via U.S. Mail on the 24th day of May, 2016, to Arizona Attorney General's Office, 400 W. Congress, Ste. 315, Tucson, Arizona 85701, attorney for Respondents.

DATED this 24th day of May, 2016.

/s/ Cedric Martin Hopkins
Cedric Martin Hopkins
Attorney for Stanford

Made in the USA
Monee, IL
13 September 2026

62979538R10090